Discovering the story of

OLD MARKET BRISTOL

Edson Burton & Michael Manson

Bristol Books CIC, 1 Lyons Court, Long Ashton Business Park,
Yanley Lane, Long Ashton, Bristol BS41 9LB

Discovering the story of Old Market, Bristol,
written and researched by Edson Burton & Michael Manson

Published by Bristol Books 2015

ISBN: 9781909446076

Copyright: Bristol Books CIC

Design: Joe Burt (joe@wildsparkdesign.com)

The authors would like to thank
all the contributors without whom this
book could not have been possible

Andrew Hurdle, BBC Radio, Delroy Hibbert, Drojan Designs, Eugene Byrne,
Fishponds Local History Society, Jonathan Taphouse, Katie Grant, Liz Lewitt,
Mandy Thomas, Martin Evans, OutStories, Rosemary Dun, Sharon Clark,
Tangent Books, Ujima Radio FM, Wild Spark Design.

The Vice & Virtue Volunteers: Alison Burrows, Christine Jones,
Elouise Kjellstad, Evanthia Triantafyllidou, Hugh Shannon, Jack Hayward,
Jenny James, Judeline Ross, Kayley Porter, Leighton De Burca,
Louise Gethin, Oliver Gamblin, Pauline Marshall, Sam Weaver,
Sara Evans, Sue Jones, Tim Jones, Zoe Gordon.

Trinity Community Arts, The Vice & Virtue Steering Group: Mal Sainsbury,
Mary Ingolby, Matthew Winterbottom, Paul Bradburn, Sarah Minter.

CONTENTS

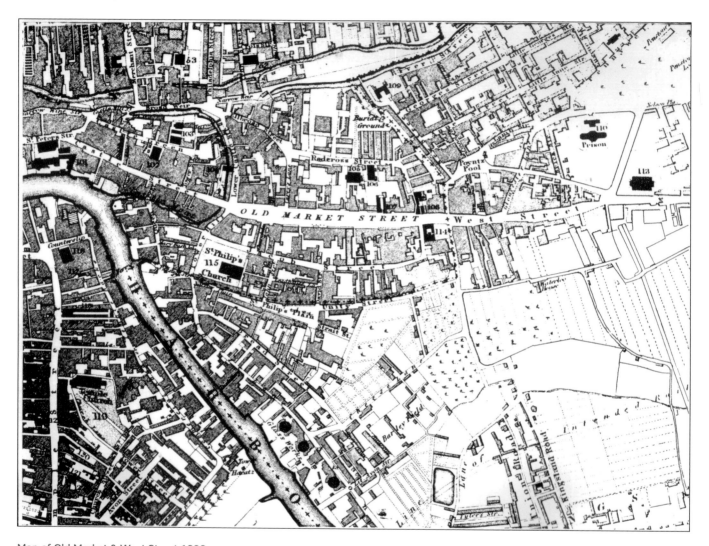

Map of Old Market & West Street 1828

INTRODUCTION

The genesis of this book began with the determination by Trinity Community Arts and the Old Market Community Association (OMCA) to excavate the history of Old Market. Previous studies, exemplary as they were, have focused on particular incidents in the life of this high street, or its industrial and architectural usage. To this end, the OMCA and Trinity Community Arts secured funding from the Heritage Lottery Fund, Quartet Foundation and the OMCA to deliver an 18-month project. Over this period we have engaged residents, employers and employees, both past and present through talks, reminiscence sessions, exhibitions, conducted group and one-to-one interviews, archival and primary research.

Honouring the wishes of our sponsors, we the authors have tried to create a more holistic picture by integrating personal recollections with the architectural and commercial story. In doing so we have been touched, warmed and enlightened by what we have learnt. We can say with confidence that Old Market is a truly remarkable street. Its journey, with its highs and lows, is one which is unique to Britain. We feel that it demonstrates the underlying ambition of our major funders - the Heritage Lottery Fund - by bringing to light forgotten corners of English Heritage.

There are a few caveats that we need to share before you begin your journey along Old Market. This is not an exhaustive study. We apologise in advance for any places, characters and themes that may have been omitted. It has simply been impossible to cover every aspect of the street's history given the length of this project and our limited resources. Please view this work as a provocation to you the reader, to correct and inform our work.

The excellent 'Know Your Place' http://maps.bristol.gov.uk/knowyourplace/ and our interactive timeline www.3ca.org.uk provide platforms for you to share additional material. A further caveat lies in our use of 'Old Market'. For the purpose of brevity our reference to Old Market includes West Street. The two are inextricably linked. The book also includes references to the wider Old Market Quarter: the area which is comprised of the Dings, Newtown, Trinity, St Matthias, Waterloo and in particular, St Judes. It is the wider quarter that contains the social history of Old Market.

The 'we' referred to in this introduction includes the many volunteers who gave their time, energy, and acumen to this research. It has been a pleasure being part of such a remarkable team. A final note of clarification: the title of the book reflects contemporary perceptions of the area. We have kept this title in order, in part, to provoke a response but more importantly to subvert the way in which the area is perceived. We ascribe neither vice nor virtue to the lives we have tried to document. They are simply part of Old Market's fascinating story.

Vice & Virtue Team

THE RISE OF OLD MARKET

Old Market Street was originally a medieval thoroughfare that led from Bristol Castle to the historic city entrance at Lawford's Gate. The Street is in the parish of St Philips. The parish church, St Philip and St Jacob, was built at the same time as Bristol Castle (1173). It was set directly outside the castle walls and, from as early as the 12th century, housed the Castle Market. Traders disputes were settled at a Market, or to give it's proper name Pied Poudre, Court. The Court convened on the site of the Stag and Hounds Inn.

Following the demolition of Bristol Castle in 1656, the area was redeveloped. Stone from the Castle is said to have been used to repave Old Market Street.[1] Several of the original 17th century building frontages remain.

Typical of market streets of that time, it was significantly wider in the middle. There were two back lanes – Redcross Street and Jacob Street (also called Back Lane according to Roche's 1750 map) – that took the traffic on market days, as this was the main road to London.[2] A number of courtyards and alleyways ran in between the two.

Millerd's 1673 map of Bristol shows the main elements of Old Market still evident today: the wide main street, the two back lanes of Redcross Street and Jacob Street and the crossroads at Lawford's Gate.

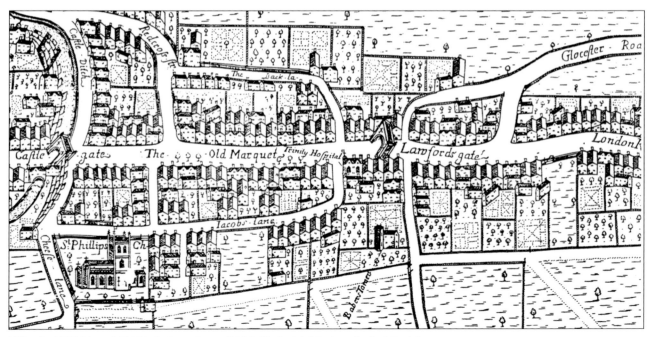

Millerd's 1673 Map of Old Market courtesy of Bristol Industrial Archaeological Society

(Top) Trinity Hospital South (FLHS)
(Bottom) Alderman Stevens Almshouse c1950s (FLHS)

VICE AND VIRTUE

'Beyond the gate' is the Bristol equivalent of the phrase 'beyond the pale.' The latter has its roots in Irish lore. It is a description of those who lived beyond the walls of Dublin Castle. As the expression implies, these folk were seen as morally questionable by the morally upright. Likewise a similar expression in Bristol 'beyond the gate' has been used to describe the men and women who lived beyond the walls of Bristol Castle.

These judgments may have arisen from the fact that, typical of medieval towns, those on the fringes of the society lived outside the city gates. For the city this alleviated the strain on the public purse: beggars could draw upon the good will of those entering and exiting the city. For the petty criminal it meant freedom from officialdom. The distinction between the inside and outside of the city walls was perhaps a self-serving one. Poverty and vice could easily be found in central Bristol, but the lawless, outsider reputation of Old Market and its immediate environs have persisted down the ages.

The association between Old Market and deprivation may also have arisen from the disproportionate number of almshouses and charities that existed in the area. The first charitable almshouse in Old Market, Trinity Hospital South, was founded by John Barstaple in 1402. He also built almshouses and a hospital opposite.

A number of other almshouses were constructed along Old Market over the years. The most significant of these was built by Alderman Stevens in 1679.

The management of the almshouses was put in the care of a new body, Bristol Municipal Properties, supposedly free from political interference in 1831. Bristol Municipal Charities took over additional properties in Old Market as a way to secure rents to support its charitable aims.

CHEEK BY JOWL

However, residents of Old Market were not all of one kind. The diversity of its populace can be seen in its architecture. Private residences of merchants and businessmen stood next to almshouses, and more simple two storey residences and shops. Built in 1706 the elegant No 59 was originally built as a private house. Its brick frontage carried on five pillars and extended over the pavement. The Stag and Hounds Inn had the same stylish design, perhaps suggesting the kind of traveller it expected to attract. Nearby, the fine bath stone façade of No 7 Redcross Street is the last surviving of a row of a classic Georgian terrace. It is better known as the birthplace of portrait painter Sir Thomas Lawrence (1769-1830).[3]

RETAIL & INDUSTRY IN PRE-19TH CENTURY OLD MARKET

The kind of businesses found along Old Market grew from its role as a thoroughfare between the rural and urban economies. Unsurprisingly, Old Market Street was a thriving centre for trade in 'flesh' and vegetables, especially on Wednesdays and Saturdays.[4] It was also home to an assortment of small industries specialising in the production and repair of farming utensils, brewers, maltsters and public houses. The sugar refinery at numbers 66-67 was one of few proto-industrial businesses in Old Market and demonstrates one of its few links to Bristol's notorious African trade. Many of Old Market's pubs and businesses have existed in the area for centuries. Rope making was another key trade - ropemakers Joseph Bryant Ltd of 95 Old Market had been in existence since 1718.[5]

Councillor Tony Dyer can trace the start of his family dynasty to the marginal community around Old Market

Joseph Orford Higgs was born in 1854 [he] and the entire family were involved largely, in wheeling and dealing. He was a hawker- they were all involved in hauliers. They were kind of like 19th century Del boys to a certain extent but later in the 19th century it became difficult, too difficult to make money on the fringes of society what had happened was..certainly by the 1830s there was now a police force in existence.[6]

Number 70 Old Market, The Long Bar, is a surviving remnant of a number of brewers, malt houses and public houses that can trace their history back to the 18th century (FLHS)

The Stag and Hounds Inn

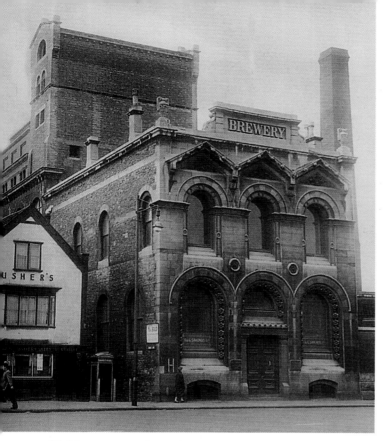

W J Rogers Brewery, Jacob Street (FLHS)

INDUSTRIAL REVOLUTION

'In the dingy district of St Philip's there are plenty of things to interest the visitor who is fond of manufactories. The whole neighbourhood pulsates with industry. In every direction you see men grimy with the marks of toil. On every hand you hear the roar of the forge, the clatter of the anvil, the thud of the steam hammer. The indescribable din of many workshops fills the air with a busy hum. All is pregnant with vitality in this smoky region.'[7]

The Industrial Revolution radically transformed Old Market and its environs. Major new businesses attracted workers from across the South West.

Among these was the Great Western Cotton Mill situated in the adjacent parish of Barton Hill. The Mill opened in 1838 with capacity for 1600 looms.

The Brewer, John Rogers established the imposing Jacob Street Brewery in 1845 at the western end of Old Market. It was reported that you could smell the yeast in the air as you got off the tram!

Hoping to take advantage of the expansion of Bristol's railway network, wine merchant John Sharp built the Palace Hotel in 1869. With a sumptuous 1860s interior with brass columns and voluptuous plasterwork, accompanied by sloping floors, the Palace Hotel was an iconic building. Great Western Railway built their main station Temple Meads, half a mile away to the South, thus somewhat disappointing John Sharp's ambitions. However the smaller St Philips railway station, opened nearby in 1870.[8]

More successfully, Christopher Thomas and Brothers opened a five storey Soap Works in Broadplain's Straight Street in 1881.

The meat trade in and around Old Market encouraged a number of ancillary industries such as the tanning works on Redcross Street and Pennywell Road plus a major hide market on West Street which supplied leather to the local boot and shoe businesses in Old Market and East Bristol generally.

Around 1920, the global meat packing firm, Swift and Company opened a branch on Braggs Lane. By innovative use of the refrigerated boxcar, Swift and Company were able to transport meat across the world.[9]

HARD TIMES

But it wasn't all brightness and cheer. Low pay and underemployment were perennial features of working class life in St Philips. 'Once-a-weekers' were among the most desperate workers – carrying out the less popular jobs such as unloading the banana boats. Some would walk from Old Market to Avonmouth in search of work.

Unskilled workers would seek employment in the docks when their trades were depressed.

Those without work could expect little from the State. Outdoor relief for a man, wife and five children was 10s 1d a week, of which rent could account for as much as 3s 6d.[10]

'THE FALLEN'

It is difficult to chart a precise history of sex work in Old Market but the early 19th century witnessed increasing concern among charitable bodies over the dangers

Amelia Elizabeth Dyer nee Hobley 1838-1896

Poverty, vice and discretion were among the ingredients which allowed the crimes of Britain's most prolific child killer to go unnoticed. Amelia Dyer was born outside Bristol in Pyle Marsh. After moving into the city she moved into lodgings on Trinity Road in 1861. Shortly afterwards she married the much older George Thomas. Dyer set herself up as a baby farmer, a woman who passed on babies born to unmarried or poor mothers who, out of shame or poverty would rather their children were adopted by more affluent families. She charged handsomely for her services. But Dyer was not interested in caring for her charges or with the matter of finding adoptive parents. Death by neglect progressed to infanticide in a criminal career that criss-crossed the South. She was eventually discovered, tried and hung in London.[11] Estimates vary, but Dyer is believed to have claimed the lives of between 300-400 victims.

The Palace Hotel more commonly known the Gin Palace after its most popular beverage. (www.flickr.com/photos/stringberd)

and hardship presented to working class women. This suggests a relationship between urbanization, poverty and sex work.

A Female Penitentiary or Magdalen House was established in 1800 for females, who, 'having strayed from the paths of virtue, desire to recover their lost character'. The Bristol Female Mission Society concentrated its efforts to 'rescue' young women, on St

Interior of a house in St Jude's (Paul Townsend twitter.com/brizzlebuff)

Judes, St James, and St Michaels. They were particularly concerned with 'preventing several young and innocent girls, who had come to Bristol in search of work, from falling into the clutches of known pimps and madams.'[12] One former resident claims that there were a number of brothels among the slums along Redcross Street furthermore that along Wade Street, the prostitutes 'wore their knickers halfway down their legs for quick access.'[13]

It seems that prostitution, then as ever, was a habitual and/or permanent means for some women to survive in times of economic hardship. But Old Market was and still remains a proud working class community. Measures taken to avoid poverty, sex work or otherwise, are not readily discussed. The lack of evidence also means that we cannot suggest whether women took up sex work as a positive choice.

THE END OF THE MARKET IN OLD MARKET

The railway added to the hustle and bustle of Old Market. Traffic increased when horse-drawn trams were introduced in June 1876, running from Old Market to Eastville, followed by an electric tramway in 1895. The west end of Old Market was used as the depot for trams going to Fishponds, Staple Hill, St.George, Hanham and Kingswood.

Unsurprisingly, the street market struggled to coexist with the tram network. The market ceased to operate during the 19th century, although some traders still sold from carts along the high street. In recognition of its decline, the Pied Poudre ceased to adjudicate in 1870,

IN MEMORY OF
RICHARD HILL.
POLICE CONSTABLE OF THIS CITY.
WHO WAS MURDERED WHILST IN THE
EXECUTION OF HIS DUTY IN GLOUCESTER LANE
24TH APRIL 1869. AGED 31 YEARS.
AND WAS INTERRED IN ARNOS VALE CEMETERY.

THIS TABLET
WAS ERECTED AS A MARK OF ESTEEM BY HIS
BROTHER OFFICERS AND INHABITANTS OF THE CITY.

"IN THE MIDST OF LIFE WE ARE IN DEATH."

SHOCKING MURDER OF A POLICEMAN AT BRISTOL.

LAW, ORDER & DISORDER IN OLD MARKET
PC Richard Hill died from wounds inflicted by William Pullin outside a pub in Old Market in 1869. Pullin hung for his crime.
Top Right: Lawford's Gate House of Correction. Opened in 1791 but no longer in use by 1860. Demolished 1907.
(twitter.com/brizzlebuff)

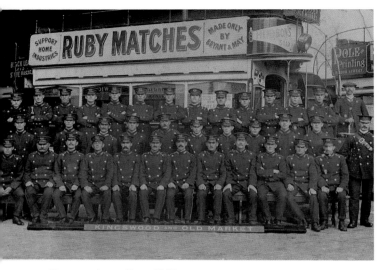

Tram workers align c1900. (Bristol Post)

but the ritual of the opening continued for another hundred years until 1970.[14] Every year on the 30th September the court was declared open but immediately adjourned.

OLD MARKET'S URBANIZATION

New opportunities for employment led to East Bristol's rapid urbanization. Rural migrants came into the city looking for work. By 1881, the population of St Philips rose from approximately 8,000 in 1801 to 50,000. Responding to ferocious demand, builders threw up homes and lodging houses as quickly and as cheaply as possible. Planning regulations, as they are now understood, were non-existent in the 19th century. Unsanitary and overcrowded conditions became the norm in the streets that ran parallel to the Old Market High Street. Homes built for two were occupied by ten. These homes lacked a proper water closet, had no drains and were supplied with water by a single tap that often served the needs of a whole court.[15] Such conditions could still be found in the 20th century. One former almshouse

resident described the dwellings along Redcross Street as 'hovels.'[16] Another former resident remembered that 'As many as ten people could be found living in the two up two down houses along Wellington Road, St Judes.'[17] The Bristol website Know Your Place provides a glimpse into the density and conditions of the local housing stock.[18] The new population increased the areas working class profile. Among the working class however, there was a wide variation in earning power between the shop owner, the artisan, the collier, the dock worker, the factory worker and the residents of the almshouses. Old Market's wealthier citizens began to drift to more affluent climes during this period. But was this was not a uniform trend.

Studies of the area at the turn of the last century reveal a diversity of trades, and households. 'The picture is one of a stable neighbourhood despite a high turnover of population.' Based on her analysis of the 1901 & 1911 census, researcher Christine Jones estimates that 62% of the local residents were born in Bristol. This corroborates the oral history testimonies that, despite its privations, generations of Bristolians had made Old Market and its environs their home. Her analysis also shows that a number of midscale employers lived above their businesses or on premises nearby.[19]

THE CIVILIZING MISSION AT HOME: CHURCH & SCHOOL

Christianity was seen as a cure for the evils that followed from rapid urbanization. It was viewed as a major civilizing force amongst the working class, discouraging vice and instilling virtue. However, St Philips and St Jacobs was the only major church in a tremendously expanded parish.

Completed in 1829, Holy Trinity Old Market was the first in a period of dynamic church building. Holy Trinity seated 1,500 and, up until post-1945, did so regularly. Further along in Braggs Lane, St Jude's the Apostle was built around 1845 on a site which may once have been used for fighting and bear baiting. These churches

created the respective, parishes of Holy Trinity and St Jude's.

The Catholic church, St Nicolas of Tolentine, opened in 1850. It served the Irish migrants – colliers and seasonal agricultural labourers – that passed through or settled in the area.

Methodism had a strong presence in St Philips. It is said that John Wesley its founder, preached his first open air sermon on April 2nd 1739, in a brick field in St. Philip's Marsh. The first Methodist Chapel in the area opened in Redcross Street in 1817. Despite a capacity for

Trinity Church 1900s

1,100 worshippers, the Chapel never quite lived up to its potential.

Thanks to the support of tobacco baron H.O. Wills II, and colliery owner Handel Cossham, the first Primitive Methodist Chapel opened in 1849 in Orchard Street, now Midland Road. The Chapel was built close to where Wesley had preached. The Ebenezer Chapel had nearly 600 seats and a schoolroom which was built in the basement for the Sunday School. Arguably, its vibrant

Bottom right: Robert Rhodes & fellow pupils. Hannah More 1962

evangelicalism was more in keeping with the local working class.[20]

One of the most active groups in St Jude's was the Bristol City Mission. The Mission was highly regarded for its work with the poor, its services and day trips. Local preacher John Couzins (1843-1918) ran an independent mission that eventually merged with the City Mission. Using funds collected from the more affluent, he provided breakfasts for the children of St Jude's as well as work for local men by establishing wood and waste paper depots.[21]

INSTRUCTION

Educational provision in Old Market, as elsewhere, was closely linked to the local churches. Hannah More School and Holy Trinity were deeply interwoven. The school was established thanks to a bequest by the Bristol philanthropist and reformer, Hannah More (1745-1833). The school was fee paying – a subscription of 1d a week was required. According to records, the reason for leaving school was often stated as 'poverty.'[22]

A school catering to the local children of Irish migrants was attached to St Nicolas of Tolentine Chuch. Built in 1905, the building on the corner of Redcross

Hannah More School

Of all the local schools, Hannah More is the most consistently and fondly remembered. Jack Williams recalls growing up as a pupil at the school.

Hannah More school was allied to Holy Trinity Church, that was their school... I attended the boys club at Hannah More school which I thoroughly enjoyed. We used to do a camp once a year. Working class kids didn't get holidays then. I was very lucky, my Dad worked in Wills, which was a good job then. At Hannah More school, the discipline was strict. If you spoke out of turn you'd get the cane... You'd go back to your seat, trying not to show a tear with the other lads and you'd have difficulty holding your pen because your fingers hurt so much...[23]

Doreen Watkins remembers class sizes of 45, attending Empire Day and Remembrance Day services plus the rivalry between Hannah More and St Nicolas of Tolentine. Former pupils also recall having to cope with the stench from the slaughterhouse behind the school on Braggs Lane.[24]

Corporal punishment was 'de rigeur' in most schools at this time. May Loveridge, a former pupil of St Nicolas and Tolentine school explained that the old formal manner and the sadistic punishments of the nuns who taught her in the 1920s led her to reject the Roman Catholic faith.[25]

Street - backing onto the newly established St Matthias Park, housed the Bristol Commercial School, specialising in secretarial skills. The schools offered practical instruction within a framework of Christian morality.

The Empire (FLHS)

SOCIAL GLUE OR SOCIAL CONTROL?

One might question the overarching reach of the various churches, their penetration into every reach of working class life. One might also see in their role a paternalism which silenced the working class. However it is also through the churches that working class men and women gained access to literacy, cut their teeth as orators, and became skilled organisers. These skills fed directly into the burgeoning labour movements.

THE EMPIRE COMES TO OLD MARKET

The entertainment firm Moss & Thornton decided to take advantage of the growth and vibrancy of the area. They opened the 2,500 capacity Empire Theatre in 1893.

The interior of the Empire was built in 'fanciful Moorish style' by architects Wylson and Long, who also designed the Winter Gardens, Blackpool. It was lit by electric light, with an auxiliary supply of gas if required. Although there was an entrance on Old Market Street, the building was tucked away down Captain Carey's Lane.

The Empire was intended to cater for the working class communities of North East & East Bristol. That said, the owners had little choice in the matter as the Theatre Royal petitioned to restrict the Empire's license to music and dancing in case it became a rival. Originally the Empire did not have a bar and patrons had to nip next door to the White Hart for a drink.

The Theatre was one Bristol's four great theatres – the others being the Bristol Old Vic, King Street; the Hippodrome, St Augustine's Parade and the Palace on Park Row.

Hopes were high but in less than a year the Empire had closed. It reopened twice but its initial demise was largely due to poor management.

OLD MARKET: THE GOLDEN YEARS 1900-1939

Old Market Street, with its transport links, entertainment centres, and range of shops, was an important and vibrant part of Bristol. The period Between 1900-1930 was marked by a series of high profile openings. Economic vitality, the impact of war and civil unrest made Old Market one of Bristol's and indeed Britain's, most dynamic High Streets. The first 30 years of the new century were the most vibrant in the street's history. This period was marked by a series of bold new developments.

KING'S CINEMA

In Bristol, as elsewhere the new medium of film transformed the possibilities for entertainment. By 1912 there were plans for the establishment of twelve picture houses in Bristol. Two of these were in Old Market.

The King's Cinema opened in 1911 under the name King's Hall on a site between Old Market and Redcross Street. Upon his return from the First World War, Ralph Bromhead bought the cinema and completed a substantial renovation involving a new frontage, a wide foyer, a low canopy outside and ornate brass work in the doors. The King's reopened in 1921 with a seating capacity of 1,500. Former residents remember the 'posh' cinema with awe.[26]

The King's was the first Cinema in Bristol to feature talking movies. In 1929 it screened the Al Jonson movie 'The Singing Fool'. Bristolians queued around the block to see the film.[27] By this time the King's had become part of the ABC Associated Cinema Chain.

The Tatler was Old Market's other major cinema. Not quiet as illustrious, it opened in 1910 on the site of what

The King's Cinema Old Market (FLHS)

was originally a roller skating rink. Situated on Carey's Lane, the Tatler could seat 800 visitors.

METHODIST CENTRAL HALL

Opened in 1924, Methodist Central Hall was the most architecturally impressive addition to Old Market's landscape.

The 19th and early 20th century was a high point for Methodism in Britain. To accommodate huge crowds, Methodists and mainly Wesleyan Methodists, built major centres of worship - 'Church Halls' - between 1886 and 1945, in most major British towns and cities. Astute evangelists, they moved away from the hierarchical ambience of traditional church to create buildings that recalled open air preaching, if not the music hall! Unable to afford a city centre location, the Methodist Conference took the decision to build a Central Hall in 1908, on the site of the under-used Old Market Wesleyan Methodist Chapel. The decision was also based on the recognition that Old Market was a focal point for work amongst the inner city poor. The original buildings were demolished and subsumed into the site of the Methodist Central Hall.

The Old Market Methodist Central Hall seated 2,000 people, with a large sweeping balcony. The ground floor fronting onto Old Market Street housed two shops and the caretakers office.

Methodist Central Hall built upon the modus operandi of Methodist evangelicalism. Through a combination of social work, entertainment and Christian fellowship, the Central Halls attracted weekly congregations in their thousands. They also provided space for philanthropic and charitable organisations. The 'Women's Bright Hour' held every Wednesday regularly attracted 2,000 women for tea, fellowship and biscuits.[28]

Former Church congregation members estimate

Methodist Central Hall (FLHS)

that as many as 2,000 young people were members of the Sunday School. To understand the appeal of the Methodists in St Philip's, one must consider the multiple crises which blighted the lives of the poor. Hunger, alcoholism and for mothers of typically large families – sheer exhaustion and depression. In these circumstances, the Methodists were able to offer material and moral salvation.[30] It was not always a choice as to whether working class men and women could have one without the other. No 7 Redcross Street, former home of the aforementioned painter Thomas Lawrence, became the base for a Medical Mission. Women were obliged to participate in hymns before they received treatment for their infections.[31]

The construction of Methodist Central Hall (FLHS)

Crowds gather to witness the opening of Central Hall and visit by the Princess Royal (FLHS)

GUILD OF THE HANDICAPPED

Old Market entered into the history books when one of Britain's first purpose built accessible buildings opened in Braggs Lane in 1913.[32] The building had been commissioned by the disabled charity, The Guild of the Brave Poor Things. Funds for 'Heritage House' were raised by its Bristol founder, Ada Vachell, the partially deaf daughter of an iron factory owner. Not just a building, Heritage House provided a centre for the isolated members of Bristol's disabled community and became a lifeline for the disabled poor. Each floor offered a range of different activities ranging from gym classes, to woodwork and reading. Bristol's Guild members were each given a bright red membership card emblazoned with their logo – a crutch crossed with a sword – and the motto 'Laetus Sorte Mea' which, translated from the Latin means 'happy in my lot.'[33] It changed its name a few years later to the Guild of the Handicapped and from

1936 was known as Guild Heritage House.

The vocabulary used by the Guild to describe their activities mirror the militarisation of British society generally on the eve of the Great War.

THE DRILL HALL

In 1912, the Old Market Sugar Refinery closed after years of slow decline. Its closure coincided with the Territorial Army's need to move from its Park Street Headquarters. Sir H.H. Willis engineered an exchange whereby the Gloucestershire Territorial Force Association were offered a new building on the site, in return for giving up their Park Street premises.'[34] The move became necessary when the newly built Municipal Art Gallery and Bristol University took up the space previously occupied by the Gloucestershire Regiment. Numbers 62 - 67 were demolished to make way for the new Hall.

Old Market Drill Hall (FLHS)

The grand opening on Wednesday 2nd June 1915 was marked by a procession from Park Street to Old Market. At the opening ceremony, Lieutenant General Bethune promised the crowd that it would never be used for any other purpose than for the good of men and Country.[35] This promise was not entirely kept. The Drill Hall was also used for dances, gatherings, became a Post Office and is now flats.

During the time it was used as primarily intended, the Drill Hall was a recruitment centre in both World Wars. In the First World War, the Hall played host to visiting US troops stationed in Salisbury, Wiltshire.

The Drill Hall also hosted troops from the Old Commonwealth, including New Zealanders.

The Hall became an addition to Old Market's thriving entertainment scene with regular dances and musical events held within its confines.

THE BRISTOL EMPIRE PALACE OF VARIETIES

The Empire does not quite fall into the category of an opening, but given it's early difficulties it is worth including in this section. The series of brief ownerships and subsequent failures continued until April 1901 when the theatre was acquired by Thomas Barrasford. Barrasford operated 19 music halls throughout the country, and was therefore able to tour the same quality acts around his circuit. Barrasford made many changes to the theatre, including improvements to the seating, the ventilation and lighting.

After its turbulent first years, the Empire began to steady under the stewardship of a seasoned music hall manager and then under resident managers, Harry

Day and Sid Macaire.[36] Thomas Barrasford began the century with a successful return to form, offering audiences an array of local, national and international variety performance staging one or sometimes two shows a night. Every conceivable act graced the Empire stage from singers such as 'Bristol's favourite' Bessie Wentworth; music hall stars Vesta Tilley, Ada Reeves; strongmen & strongwomen Atlas and Miss Vulcana; hypnotists and comedians such as the Funniest Man on Earth and Little Tich; dancers, magicians and escapologists including the renowned Harry Houdini and a combination of all of the above. In 1909 the Empire even hosted a boxing kangaroo!

Variety acts were a way for Bristol working class audiences to experience the wider world, albeit in an often crude, jaundiced and distorted fashion. These performances tell us much about attitudes to race and difference at the time. September 1900 saw a performance by Eugene Stratton the 'greatest coon delineator'. Similarly, internationally famous 'black face' performer G.H.Elliot was a hit with Empire audiences in 1902. Octoroon sisters Colie and Mamie Grant also

Angela Tuckett

Angela Tuckett was one of a number of prominent women activists associated with the Hall. Bristol's only female solicitor, Tuckett demonstrated a lifelong commitment to radical politics. She vigorously supported the Welsh contingent of the 1931 Hunger Strike - she brought food and copies of the 'Daily Worker ' to the march every day.

Angela later joined the Communist party. She travelled widely before she and her sister Joan became involved in setting up Bristol's Unity Theatre.[37]

Cary Grant

In 1917, a young Archie Leach (Cary Grant) operated the limelights at The Empire.[38] As well as his fine acting, Cary Grant was also known for his impeccable transatlantic accent. But according to a fellow schoolmate, young Archie spoke with a broad Bristol accent during his youth.[39]

(Bristol Post)

Kingsley Hall - the home of the left in Bristol.

KINGSLEY HALL

Bristol East was, and still is, a labour stronghold. Most notably Labour giant Stafford Cripps was elected in a by-election for Bristol East in 1931. Located between the city's centre and its outlying Eastern suburbs, Old Market was a perfect meeting point for working class political activists. Both sides of the political spectrum competed for the hearts and minds of the working classes of East

came to the Empire in 1906. A troupe of Japanese artists presented an 'Elaborate Display of Draperies and Costumes' while 'Twenty Genuine Negroes' starred in a show 'A trip to Coon Town'. Freak shows included Johnny Trundley the 'Peckham Fat Boy', Smaun Sing Hpoo the '34 inch tall Burmese midget' and the conjoined sisters - 'The Bohemia Twins', billed in April 1904.[40]

Current affairs also dictated what appeared on stage. In 1900 singer Kate Carney dedicated the song 'Only a Bugler Boy' to a Boer War hero, a trumpeter named Sherlock. Shows such as 'Trafalgar' 'Battlefield Bess' and 'The Ten Tommies' reflected the real life events of the First World War, attempting tried to rouse the collective spirits as casualties began to mount.

By the turn of the century, moving pictures began to vie with the music hall for the attention of the British Public. The Empire, like many other entertainment venues began to accommodate and indeed benefit from cinema's popularity. By 1912, the Empire had begun to include film screenings in between its twice nightly evening bills.[41]

One of its ventures into film was the screening of the silent masterpiece 'The Loves of Pharaoh' (1923). The screening was accompanied by a live orchestra and was a spectacular hit with Bristolians.[42]

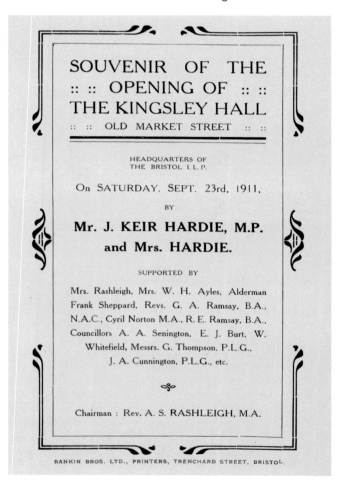

SOUVENIR OF THE
:: :: OPENING OF :: ::
THE KINGSLEY HALL
:: :: OLD MARKET STREET :: ::

HEADQUARTERS OF
THE BRISTOL I.L.P.

On SATURDAY, SEPT. 23rd, 1911,

BY

Mr. J. KEIR HARDIE, M.P.
and Mrs. HARDIE.

SUPPORTED BY

Mrs. Rashleigh, Mrs. W. H. Ayles, Alderman Frank Sheppard, Revs. G. A. Ramsay, B.A., N.A.C., Cyril Norton M.A., R. E. Ramsay, B.A., Councillors A. A. Senington, E. J. Burt, W. Whitefield, Messrs. G. Thompson. P.L.G., J. A. Cunnington, P.L.G., etc.

Chairman : Rev. A. S. RASHLEIGH, M.A.

RANKIN BROS. LTD., PRINTERS, TRENCHARD STREET, BRISTOL.

Souvenir of the opening of Kingsley Hall 1911. (Bristol Central Library)

Bristol. In 1906, John Lysaght established the St Philip's Conservative Club for the benefit of working men at No 59 Old Market. No 59 named the hall 'Salisbury Hall' after the Conservative leader. The purpose of the club was to do everything it could to 'contribute to their social improvement'. The Conservative presence did not last long however. A tide of working class radicalism swept through the country in the run up to the First World War.[43]

Having outgrown their offices in Stokes Croft, the Independent Labour Party (ILP) procured No 59 Old Market. The building was renovated to include a new meeting room at the back.[44] Renamed after the Christian Socialist, historian, priest and novelist Charles Kingsley (1818-1875), the building was reopened in 1911 by Mr and Mrs Kier Hardie. Kier Hardie was one of the founders of the ILP. His wife Lillias was a celebrated organiser amongst the women's union movement. The programme notes of the event include the proclamation that Kingsley Hall should be 'the home of the working class movement in all its phases.'[45] The profile of the event and what was to follow demonstrate the importance of Kingsley Hall and Old Market generally to the Labour Movement.

A number of Trade Union organisations took up offices in Kingsley Hall or in premises nearby including the Amalgamated and Engineering Union; Amalgamated Society of Woodcutting Machinists; British Railwayman's Club and Institute; National Society of Painters; National Union of General and Municipal Workers and the self-styled Trade Union Organizer Harry Webb.

Kingsley Hall also reflected the national growth in union activity among women. The National Union of General Worker's section held an office in Kingsley Hall. The Women's Section of the Central Labour Party met on the first Thursday of every month and The National Federation of Women Workers also held regular meetings at the Hall.[46]

The Hall was used for fundraising and social activities including dances, music, whist drives and clothing sales.

Central Hall was a popular venue for classical music. Visitors included the Royal Philharmonic Orchestra. 1965 (FLHS)

Indeed in 1921 the United Irish League wanted to hold a dance and whist drive at the Hall on St Patrick's Day.

Kingsley Hall was not the only venue for radical meetings in Old Market. The Bristol Socialist Society (1885 – 1941) met throughout the winter on Sunday evenings at Shepherd's Hall.

SHEPHERD'S HALL

Presaging the explosion in working class self organisation, Shepherd's Hall opened in Old Market in 1889. The Hall was built by the architects Foster and Wood (Colston Hall, Grand Hotel, Foster's Almshouses & Co) on behalf of the Loyal Order of Ancient Shepherds. The Order was a self help organisation formed by working class men in North West England to assist each other in times of financial hardship. The Order spread across the country through a lodge system. Bristol's lodge opened in 1851. For many years Shepherd's Hall was the venue for worker's meetings, speeches, and fund-raising events. Tony Benn was one of many left wing luminaries to visit the Hall.[47]

The meetings were not entirely devoted to serious political debate. Families would attend and the gatherings would finish with singing and piano playing.[48]

The Empire Music Hall was also a venue for Socialist meetings.[49] Another Labour luminary Ben Tillett was also actively involved with the hall.[50] Tillet, a founding father of the Trade Union Movement spoke at the Hall on numerous occasions.[51]

ROSEMARY NURSERY

The opening of Rosemary Street Nursery in St Jude's was another historic occasion in the rich life of the area. The nursery was supported by the local Quakers but the driving force behind its creation was a local woman of humble origin, Ellen King (1897-1968). Orphaned from the age of 10, Ellen went on to become its first Headmistress when the nursery opened in 1925.[52]

SHOPPING IN OLD MARKET HIGH STREET

'We used to ...Go for a walk... down to Old Market, up Castle Street, possibly on from there to the Downs and back again.'[53]

The variety of shops in Old Market increased in line with the growth of the population and the opportunities

---

Shops, Hostelries and other Retail Services in Old Market in 1901

- For food needs there were butchers (4), bakers (2), grocers (4), fruiterers (2), wine and spirit merchants (3), confectioners (5) and a fish merchant.
- There were eight pubs, one temperance bar, a coffee house and a dining room.
- For health matters there were two surgeons and one chemist.
- Clothing could be obtained from two outfitters, a glover, a hatter and two boot makers. There was just one hairdresser. Also a pawnbroker – Raselle's.
- There were also two photographers, an ironmonger, and a newsagent.
- Although the majority of premises were occupied by retailers, there were also two mineral water manufactures and four watch makers.
- The District Inland Revenue maintained an office in

Old Market Street as did the Registry Office.
- The Bristol Tramways and Carriage Company also had a passenger waiting room and a branch office in the street.
- There were no banks in Old Market Street – though there were two small branch banks in West Street.
- Old Market's retail profile altered by 1930 in line with changing public tastes. There was a drop in food sellers but an increase in tobacconists; the two boot makers had closed – probably unable to compete with the larger manufacturers in Soundwell and Kingswood. The mineral water manufactories had closed. The four watchmakers were now whittled down to just one watchmender. There was now a garage and two shops selling bikes.[54] By 1931, the nine pubs in the street had increased to ten when a wine and spirit merchant became The Punchbowl. The Temperance Bar had closed and there were now five Refreshment Rooms.

Raselle's

One of the streets longest serving shops was Raselle's the pawnbroker. The three Gold balls over the frontage were unmistakable. For Britain's poor it was not uncommon to pawn their Sunday best on Monday in the hope of buying them back by Sunday.[55] Based in Old Market, for three generations Raselle's was one of Bristol's most notable pawnbrokers. Amos Raselle lived in Lancashire Road, Bishopston and attended St Michael of All Angels Church on Pigsty Hill – now demolished. Amos Raselle died on 15 April 1935. The shop continued to be run under his name:

> Amos Raselle had a pawnbroker's shop in Old Market opposite the Almshouses and Jacob Street. Amos always wore a black astrakhan coat and a small round astrakhan hat. He was about five feet tall with a little goatee beard and looked very much like King Edward VII and was known as a friend to the poor. As his business was founded amongst the poor and needy in St. Philips and places like that, he was well known. For instance in the School Emanuel, (a Church of England School which I attended) every year at the annual prize giving a considerable amount of prizes, which were usually books, were purchased with a donation from Amos. He often visited our school, everyone knew him. We kids thought he was marvellous because he always tried in our hearing to get the Headmaster to let us off early that day. Though Mr. Raselle had ceased trading there for some time, the shop that bore his name still existed in the 1980s. Post World War One, things were really rough. A young cousin of mine was really hard up. They had a large family and his father had not worked since the war. Now,

> Amos presented the school with a gold watch for the best boy in the school, academically the best boy. My cousin won it. A gold watch in a family with about seven kids and an unemployed father would not have a long life but this one did. It went into Amos' pawnbroker's shop and out again every week until 1935 when conditions began to improve.[56] 〞

Legend has it that Adge Cutler, front man with The Wurzel's, kitted out the band with corduroy trousers bought from Raselles. The story goes that Adge purchased the trousers first and then looked for band members to fit them.[57]

(FLHS)

No 42 Old Market Butlers Chemist. Local medicine in the form of an apothecary, druggist, or chemist has existed on the High street since the 18th century. (FLHS)

that emerged from its location.

By 1900, Old Market was part of the 'golden mile' of streets that stretched from Lawrence Hill to the city centre. Visitors came from near and far drawn by the variety of shops. Old Market catered for almost every requirement.[58]

It was such a lucrative area for retail that, as one firm closed another would take its place. Visitors to the street during this 'golden era' point out that anything and everything one might require could be found along Old Market. Some of these shops and firms hold the key to the streets history.

At the beginning of the 20th century, Old Market Street, with its tram terminus, shops, churches and the Empire theatre was a bustling thoroughfare used by people coming into Bristol from the newly developed suburbs to the east of the city including Easton, St George, Fishponds and Mangotsfield. Underground toilets were an additional incentive for those travelling into the area to stop off at Old Market..

RADICAL & UNRULY: OLD MARKET UNEMPLOYMENT RIOTS 1932

Situated between the city and East Bristol with its collieries and factories, Old Market has been the site of protest and conflict. In 1889, factory operatives, mostly women, at the Barton Hill Cotton Factory came out on strike for higher wages and better conditions. They paraded day after day from the factory gate through Old Market to the city centre and Clifton.[59]

Even the children of Old Market were insurrectionary. There were school strikes in Bristol in October 1889, September 1911 and October 1914. In October 1914 a strike was organised in St Jude's school protesting against the exploitation of monitors. Pupils also tried to involve colleagues from Hannah More School. It was quickly quashed and the ringleader, Sam Brick, was given the cane – 'three lashes on each hand.'[60]

The First World War suspended a period of civil unrest in Britain brought on by class and political division. The 1929 Wall Street Crash reignited deep seated tensions in Britain. Bristol, as elsewhere, was hit hard by the Great Depression which followed the crash. Nearly 2,000 people registered at one of the six labour exchanges across the city. The people of St Philips were particularly affected by the Depression. Two major local employers – the Great Western Cotton Works and the Bristol Carriage Works - had closed with the loss of several thousand jobs. The most precarious forms of employment, such as along the docks became even more insecure.

In Old Market, working and church organisations rallied together to support hard pressed men and women protesting against unemployment. West Street Congregational Church ran an Unemployed Men's Club. In 1932, they held a Christmas party that involved music, singing, games of skittles and the distribution, to married men, of meat and mince pies.[61]

In 1936, 500 Welshmen marching to London were billeted in a number of places across the city including

Old Market St., Bristol. (4)

The hustle and bustle of Old Market (FLHS)

Kingsley Hall and the Central Methodist Hall.[62]

Not all workers organisations were so enamoured of the marchers. The Bristol Unemployed Association, based in Kingsley Hall, announced in the Western Daily Press that it was in no way connected with other associations that were bringing unemployed marchers into the city.[63]

Despite efforts such as the 'Unity Campaign,' the workers movement splintered on ideological grounds.[64] Indeed the ILP documents from Kingsley Hall reveal the split between the Independent Labour Party and the Labour Party in 1932.[65] Unions or parties did not have automatic control over the movement. The then coalition Government feared that Communists were destabilising the country. Protest marches in Bristol and elsewhere seemed to suggest that this was indeed the case. The Government were particularly concerned by the activities

of The National Unemployed Workers Union (NUWU). The NUWU struggled for the support and recognition by the Trade Union Movement.[66] They organised a march on Pancake Day 1932, which led to what have been called the Old Market Riots.

On the 29 January 1932, the Public Assistance Committee, who were responsible for administering unemployment relief, reduced unemployment benefit by 10%.

To protest against this cut in assistance, the National Unemployed Workers Union (NUWU) proposed a march to the Council House, which was at that time on the corner of Corn Street and Broad Street. The police however, forbade the protesters to approach the Council House and re-routed the march in the opposite direction towards Old Market.[67]

At Old Market, the police attempted to divert the crowd down Carey's Lane - next to the King's Cinema. due to the sheer number of the crowd, - between 4,000 and 5,000 people,[68] the police were jostled. The Chief Constable gave the order for batons to be drawn and the protestors charged.

Inspector Dyke, the policeman in charge at the scene, reported that: *'sticks with nails protruding were being thrown at and used upon the police. I then gave instructions to the men who arrived with me to clear the street. The crowd was very hostile and it was impossible for any traffic to get away until the crowd was dispersed by the policemen using their sticks.'*[69]

Inevitably, some bystanders were injured. One eye-witness reported: *'The police on mounted horses and other police with batons charged us and drove us back into Old Market Street. Oh yes, people got hurt, people who weren't even in the scuffle. I can remember... a little lady there, there were a man and a woman there, they were clubbed down. They said they had just come from the pictures. And they had nothing to do with it.'*[70] One policeman and several protesters were seriously injured though no arrests were made.

The dispersed crowd regrouped at the Horsefair where speeches were delivered. Police reinforcements from the nearby Bridewell Police Station were called and the demonstrators dispersed. Two people were arrested for disorderly conduct and assaulting police officers.

Some people felt that the police had been too heavy handed. Councillor H. E. Rogers (Bristol East Divisional Labour Party) wrote to Chief Constable Maby demanding disciplinary action be taken against the police for using

unjustified violence. *'Surely your men have not been instructed to trample to death law-abiding citizens whose only object is to pursue the legitimate conduct of citizens!'*[71] The Watch Committee concluded, however, that the police had acted with 'commendable restraint'.[72]

Two weeks later, despite being refused permission by the police to march, the NUWU led another protest. Again the march ended at Old Market Street. The South Gloucester Gazette reported:

'At the unemployed headquarters at Shepherds Hall, over which continually floats the Red flag, a posse of police barred the way. For a time the crowd halted, but eventually, urged on from the back, it advanced again, and the police drew batons in readiness. Immediately came a shower of missiles, half-bricks, coke, gas-piping and iron bars, all of which had been collected by the procession en route. Immediately the police charged and in a moment the demonstrators were scattering in all directions, those who stood their ground being speedily dealt with. Again and again the police swept through their ranks and two ambulances were soon busy carrying casualties to the Infirmary.'[73]

Bill Curtis, a participant, saw things differently:

'To the right hand side as we were facing Castle Street... in the annex to the Empire Theatre...he (Chief Constable Maby) had two more motor coach loads of police there in reserve ... hiding in the annex and the theory was that if they came out from the annex and took the first dozen rows from behind they'd have the ring leaders and all the march would break up into disorder... which he wasn't very far wrong... these other police piled out from the annex and took us from behind... and of course right away you know a punch up started, people

was getting whacked with the batons... we was getting a right licking...'[74]

According to Bill Curtis the demonstrators grabbed anything that was at hand to use as missiles. Market stalls were raided and potatoes, cabbages and coal was thrown at the police.

Photographs of the demonstration show policemen with truncheons beating marchers to the ground. Several bodies lie sprawled on the road, bicycles abandoned, placards discarded. At a press conference the next day, Chief Constable Maby justified this brutal containment with a display of weapons - jemmies, batons, metal railings - allegedly taken from the protesters. He claimed that no more than 50 police men were engaged in dispersing demonstrators. The Bristol Evening World however, reported that nearly 300 police took part.

By now the disturbances in Bristol had drawn the attention of the Home Office, who made a 'telephonic inquiry' about the events.

Maby's subsequent report to the Home Office appeared to be more concerned with the interruption to the traffic than anything else. Maby succinctly described the events in Old Market:

'One procession proceeded through St Philips down Old Market Street, and another procession, at the same time, marched from the other end of Old Market Street. Causing serious congestion. A cordon of police was immediately lined up across Old Market Street and the marchers requested to stop. They refused and were told they would not be allowed to march any further and must disperse. The marchers then attacked the police with sticks and banners, pieces of iron, stones and other missiles and the inspector in charge gave orders for the police to draw their truncheons and disperse the crowd, and after a short time order was restored. The mounted police were called out, but did not draw their staves.'[75]

The protests continued throughout the spring of 1932. The police were less heavy handed, preferring to monitor the situation rather than wade in. Meanwhile, Chief Inspector Maby opened up correspondence with his counterpart in Manchester, Chief Constable Maxwell, where similar disturbances had occurred in Stevenson Square.

On the 13 April 1932, Maby wrote to Maxwell: 'I believe that time has come to say 'stop' and proceedings are therefore being instituted against some of the communist speakers.'[76]

Just down the road from Old Market, on Friday 10 June, the police organised an 'ambush' of demonstrators in Castle Street. 15 people were treated at the Royal Infirmary and another two at the General Hospital.[77] Three men, Bailey, Webber and Parker were charged and found guilty of 'inciting persons to assault the police'. They were sentenced to six months and six months and a year, respectively.[78]

Fortunately the unemployment situation began to improve. By 1937 there were only 11,500 people registered as unemployed in Bristol. It was boom time again, largely helped by the rise of the aeroplane manufacturing industry.

The ferocity of the Old Market Riot captured in this iconic picture (FLHS)

THE SECOND WORLD WAR 1939 – 1945

ristol's historic City Centre was decimated during the Bristol Blitz: Nazi bombers flattening both Castle and Vine Street.

Although bomb damage to Old Market was relatively minimal, the area was certainly aware of the bombings. 'One of the [air raid] sirens, the nearest one, was on top of the police station at Trinity Road.'[79] Nearby, Rosemary Street Nursery was also used as an air raid shelter. Only Nos. 1- 4 were destroyed, while the roof of Stevens Almshouse suffered damage from an incendiary device.[80] The goods yard at St Philips Station however, was badly bombed.

Age and proximity to destruction play a vital role in understanding the contrasting memories of the blitz.[81]

Antony Peplar recounted his grandmother's experience of:

'Being at Church [Central Hall] when the 1940 air raids happened and sheltering in the crush until they got the all-clear and having to pick her way back through the rubble to get home to her parents house in Totterdown.'[82]

Frightening as this may seem V.A Hole remembers that:

'To a large extent, strange as it might seem, the war was a kind of entertainment for children. The next morning after an air raid you'd go out shrapnel hunting which was the residue of shells, bombs... as children you played in the street..so the war to a lot of children was a kind of entertainment because you weren't aware of the implications of it...'[83]

Charley Plenty was one of many local residents who experienced the disruption to family life caused by war time evacuation. His older siblings were evacuated to

Cornwall during the war but he and his sisters, being very young, stayed at home with his mother.[84]

The bombing of Goodhind Street and Newfoundland Street took the lives of local residents and brought the realities of war even closer. A plaque on the side of St Peter's Church commemorates the loss of five fire watchers. Holloway, Kennan, Compton, Sparks and Martin were all local men who lost their lives in service to the community.[85]

In fits and starts life carried on through the War. Indeed the Empire benefited to some extent from the damage to the Colston Hall and Prince's Street Theatre. War time entertainment at the Empire was designed to keep up morale. The 'Naughty' theme ruled, as one can discern from the titles of shows such as 'Don't Blush Girls', 'Step out with Phyllis,' 'Bearskins and Blushes' and 'Fiddle-de-Dee' featuring the scantily clad cartoon strip hero Jane.

As well as imported acts, local performers and wannabes sought to capitalise on their military audiences. Blessed in his youth with a fine voice, Jack Williams remembers:

'One of our friends who was a little bit older than us, he said you're good, why don't you come with me on a Sunday night when the American troops are being entertained by local people down at the Empire theatre, but none of my mates would come. He imitated Danny Kaye,... that's what he did, that was his speciality this young lad and he was good.'[86]

Given the damage to Bristol's other theatre's, the Central Hall was much in demand. Trustees allowed the use 'provided it generally be known that we are a Church

Family Tragedy

Tony Dyer's family maintained close links with Old Market despite moving out of the area to the new suburbs of Knowle. With the outbreak of war, Joseph Higgs promised his sisters that he would look after Great Uncle Stan' when they joined the army. To make good on this promise, brothers aimed to enlist in the Somerset Light Infantry:

> *They were indeed placed in the Light Infantry but in two different units - the 1st 4th Battalion of the King's Yeoman Light Infantry and the 1st Battalion of the Oxford and Bucks Light Infantry.*
>
> *Obviously D-Day was coming up and they were called away to their different units... my great Uncle landed on Sword Beach... he was attached to the 6th group. Their job was to help clear away the mines and obstructions to allow the troops to come through... Four days later... my Grandad landed with his unit on Gold Beach. In a cruel twist of fate the two brothers passed each other. Grandad saw Stan and we assume he saw him. That was the last time they saw each other because on either the 1st or 2nd of August 1944 Great Uncle Stan was clearing some mines and one of 'em exploded and killed him - he left a 19 year old widow. It was a long time before my Grandad would talk about having met him. He felt he had not kept his promise to look after Great Uncle Sam.*[87]

and expect to be treated as such.'[88]

But all venues were subjected to the dictates of war. The Empire had to close for a week at a time during the Blitz. It was also difficult for its owners to find materials to repair the fabric of the building.

GUM, SEGREGATION, & CONDOMS: US SERVICE IN OLD MARKET

Between 1942 and 1945, about 3 million US servicemen were stationed in Britain for varying lengths of time. The largest number gathered in the South West. When the first troops sailed into Avonmouth in August 1942, they were met with a rapturous reception.[89]

Better paid than British squaddies and armed with a New World swagger, American servicemen made a seismic impact on Bristol. Young men away from home and preparing for War, the Americans found entertainment in the bars and pubs across the City including Old Market.

A number of local women were drawn to the newcomers:

'I was escorted to the King's Cinema by an American soldier to see 'The Glenn Miller Story.' The accents of the GI servicemen and the scent of their cigars added to the novelty and pleasure of the films.'[90]

'It seemed as though it was the craze to me... to get an American. And some of them left their husbands for Americans.'

...I suppose they had more to give. They had more money, and used to give us meat and stockings – nylons. You wouldn't get that from an Englishman. They treated the women good, they really did.'[91]

One woman remembers queuing for hours at an American Army base in Bedminster for chewing gum and ice cream.[92]

COLOUR CLASH

But romance exacerbated tensions in America's 'Jim Crow' Army. Black servicemen made up 10% of the US Army. Split along racial lines, the US army insisted on maintaining or rather exporting its strict code of segregation into Europe. This was frowned on in Britain, but tolerated. Privately Winston Churchill described the situation as 'certainly unfortunate.'

In Bristol, Black troops were billeted, initially in the Old Market Street Drill Hall, then Bedminster, Brislington, Henleaze, Shirehampton and the Muller Orphanage at Ashley Down.[93]

Right to left Bill & Albert. Becky Mighty went on to marry Bill.

Either officially or unofficially, pubs and other facilities such as fish and chip shops became segregated. The Black GIs claimed that they were unfairly confined to barracks and were only allowed into the less salubrious parts of Bristol.

The personal testimony of Theodora Mighty, a Bristolian of mixed heritage, corroborates the segregation against American troops:

'The GIs were treated badly in Bristol. There were lots of pubs they couldn't go into. And people wouldn't give them places to live. They lived in the barracks...'

She further explained:

'To come into town with them, you couldn't go into town... the Spread Eagle, black people used to go there, and there was another one on St Michael's Hill... St Davids pub was it? On the corner of St Michael's Hill, and then a bit further up there was another called the Eglington (Upper Maudlin Street –later called the Sea Horse), and the Black people took over these pubs and we all got on well together. If you knew you wanted to
meet *a Black soldier you knew where to go. They sort of took over, because they knew they couldn't just go to any pub. They had a hard time really.'*

As the extract above suggests, relationships did develop between British women and African American soldiers.

Officially, it was the task of the American Military Police to enforce the Colour Bar but anecdotes from the time suggest a more complex picture.

'I remember when I was in the army, walking along the Centre, with a white girl, we were both in uniform and the military police stopped us and said to me 'you know you're not supposed to be out with Black Americans – and there's me, mixed race! They were [the Red Caps] the British police. The Red Caps. Yeah, they stopped me and reported me.'[94]

Relationships between White women and Black men were unthinkable in the Southern States of the USA. In Britain the unthinkable happened. This and the general

The Drill Hall where Black troops were initially billeted.

refusal by Black service men to accept second-class citizenship antagonised their White counterparts.

The Chief Constable of Bristol, C.G. Maby, wrote a memo on 7 October 1942:

'*Several cases have occurred recently of altercations between American troops and members of the public and between coloured troops and seamen. Women are also alleged to have been accosted. It is pointed out that it is the duty of the police to maintain public order and decency in the streets and whilst these troops are not amenable to English law, it does not follow that they cannot offend against our laws. If unseemly conduct is observed in such circumstances which do not justify the persons being arrested, such as producing knives or other offensive weapons, urinating in the public carriageway, and causing disturbances at dances and public meetings, steps must be taken to deal with the matter in the same way as the civilian population is dealt with. Names and addresses should be taken if possible of the parties concerned and any other information which may be useful to forward to the American Authorities in order that appropriate action can be taken. Police Officers must maintain their authority with tact and discretion, irrespective of the class of person with whom they have to deal.'*

The Americans divided opinion:
'*Dad never liked the Americans.*'
Why's that?
'*He was a communist, actually. He was right against the Americans in those days. I remember he used to belong to the Labour Party... he always told me the Americans were no good at all. All this sort of stuck in my mind, but I don't have anything against the Americans, you know, in those days. Like I always thought they come across with the goodies, and that was good, and we used to like that, you know.*'[95]

For the most part the Americans returned home after the War, some leaving behind 'brown babies.' Occasionally local women followed their American lovers to the States. A degree of normality returned to Old Market but the Street was never the same again.

Racial tension comes to Old Market

White GIs would visit the pubs and clubs frequented by Black servicemen looking for a fight. In Old Market the Spread Eagle pub was a favourite haunt of Black service men. True to form there are stories of fights spilling out into Old Market Street and West Street.[96]

❝ *I remember when they had a real skirmish in Old Market once. .. coming back [from the Kings Cinema] we had to go through all the fighting 'cos the Americans sort of getting at each other 'cos sort of in those days it was Black and White, and it was terrible.*[97] *The Bristol Police never got into it at all. The GIs... they came and sorted it out. And we got up on the pavement. I was terrified, I was, that night.*[98] ❞

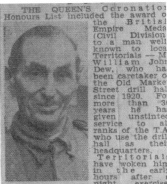

THE QUEEN'S Coronation Honours List included the award of the British Empire Medal (Civil Division) to a man well known to local Territorials — Mr William John Dew, who had been caretaker of the Old Market Street drill hall since 1920. For more than 30 years he had given unstinted service to all ranks of the T.A. who use the drill hall as their headquarters.

Territorials have woken him in the early hours after a night exercise and have seen him waiting to lock up after a late party; but they have never found him less than good humoured. To members of the 44/50th Royal Tank Regiment, who now have the drill hall as their "home." Mr Dew is a never-failing source of advice and ready service.

Mr Dew is now 61. He joined the 2nd Battalion Grenadier Guards in 1912 and, was severely wounded on the Somme in 1916. He was dis...

**Photographs of St Phillips, & Barton Hill service personnel. Top left: distant relatives anonymous courtesy of Susan Green.
Bottom left: third from left, Richard Dunn. Top & bottom right: War veteran W.J.Dew** (Lynn Mitchell)

OLD MARKET AFTER THE SECOND WORLD WAR 1946-1967

Popular local wisdom suggests that Old Market's decline can be traced to the post war period. Research for this book suggests that Old Market's fortunes went up and down after the work and should be considered on a decade-by-decade basis.

Bristol breathed a 'sigh of relief' after the War.'[99] But across the city, including in Old Market, life did not return to 'normal' immediately. Essential food items were still subject to rationing.

Former local residents Norman Gauter, Bob and Moira recall:

Bob Jones: *'We used to, we used to have butter, and we used to fight over the butter. We all had a saucer each, and my Mum cut up our ration of butter and we had the butter on the saucer.'*

Norman: *'And I used to spit on mine, so no one would eat from it.'*[100]

It was not until 1954 that rationing was lifted on all items.

The impact of rationing was perhaps even more acute after the war: *'we'd been used to rationing all through the War but it didn't get any better. It was almost worse at the end of the war cause, well, the men had come back so there were more people but there wasn't more food available.'*[101]

Britain's readjustment after the war is understated. Some demobbed soldiers found it difficult to return to employment.

'Where I worked in David's, [general store in Old Market] which was a wholesale company at that time there were what we call pedlars or door to door salesmen where they used to go around with a little suitcase and I mean little as well, stuck with everyday articles in and they knock on doors and they sell what they can in that case so the next morning they would have to go and sell what they had in that case again...we dealt with a lot of those people..so everyday they would buy their little pieces...fill up their suitcase and off they go, there were some older people, but they were mostly people from the War who didn't know what to do, what job to do so they were doing that. They must have been struggling because if they sold everything every day they were still gonna hardly make anything.'[102]

Hawkers became less of a familiar sight along Old Market as most of these returning soldiers found their way into regular work. The post-war years were marked by an unprecedented employment boom. 'There was

Freda Rhodes & George Higgins

From Local Store to Arts Cafe

Up to his adolescence Robert Rhodes worked in the family shop in West Street 'there were so many, many characters there both from people who lived in the area because there were still lots of people who lived in the area or had business... and there was quite a social thing in the shop y'know people would come in and there would be... talk going on, banter sometimes, rows... it would be the sort of place where people would come and they would actually come not just to do their shopping but to sit and talk with my mum and my gran. They'd be there for 2-3 hours... Almshouses were still almshouses then for people who couldn't afford to live anywhere else. I remember, at Christmas, making-up parcels to be delivered for their Christmas provision. It was very much a community then.'

Robert also remembers 'a drinking contest at the Gin Palace between two men who could drink the most Worthington E and I remember the winner being carried out by a great throng of people.' At some point in his youth 'across the road, for want of a better word across the road was Hells Angels hangout run by Greek Cypriots... there was always some cabaret going on with the police coming round but it was always good naturedly.[103]

certainly no problem with getting work' said one local employee.[104]

The privations and sacrifices, the exposure to new ideas led many working class men and women to question the values of British society. The Central Hall's 1947 Anniversary Report observed:

'Only a minority of the young men and women who left us for the Forces have returned to work and worship with us... Some have gone to live elsewhere... A great number are tired and disillusioned.'[105]

But it would be precocious to suggest that the rapid decline in Church attendance can be traced to this period, or indeed that this decline was caused by a growth in atheistic tendencies. This came much later during the 1960s. Church attendance remained a critical part of the cultural life of St Philips. Indicating a confidence unlikely today. The Central Hall's minister Phillip Odell mounted a sterling campaign to replace the numbers lost after the War. He targeted, in particular, the young. Audrey Dayer remembers:

'One minister... Reverend Odell he noticed on a Saturday night young people just aimlessly walking about with nothing much to do and they put a notice up in the paper to bring your best boy or best girl to the Central Hall on a Saturday for Youth club, price six pence with refreshments.'[106]

The call was successful.

In the 1950s and 60s the Vicars of Holy Trinity, Frederick John Barff and John Alexander Motyer drew crowds and created programmes.[107] Furthermore, the Ebenezer Chapel on Midland Road reopened as a Christadelphian Hall in 1952.

St Jude's Church continued to play a vital role in the life of its parishioners. Local vicar Father White was remembered with particular fondness by residents:

'Vicars were social workers in those days, so if you had any problems, personal or family problems, there was no social workers, you went to the local vicar...and obviously there was a lot of petty crime and husbands and sons was always bein' interviewed by the police and he was the first [in the courts] and if anybody died he was first there to lay them out and prepare them.'[108]

GOLDEN TWILIGHT

The youthful recollections of many of the interviewees for this book are drawn from this period. They recall an area

Buses, cars, bikes and people compete in bustling Old Market,
Saturday 9th Feb 1946 (Bristol Record Office)

which in the 1950s and 60s was very much alive. Young
and old could find all their entertainment needs met in Old
Market.

Young people also had a choice of entertainment
'Tom and Jerry, Superman, Supergirl, Batman, Cowboys
and Injuns - at the King's Cinema, the News Cinema on
Castle Street or the cheaper and less salubrious Vestry
Hall described locally as the 'Bug House' on account of its
insect inhabitants.'[109]

Anderson's fairground provided entertainment all year
round. The fairground was situated on a stretch of land
off Midland Road - known in local parlance as 'the Batch.'
Bob Jones remembers that: 'As teenagers we went

Local Perks

Local firms contributed to an informal economy. In
true Old Market fashion, Norman Gautier struck up a
deal with his fellow posties and a local butcher:

> *Every Friday, we`d all go up with our orders,
> from their wives, their chops, their sausages,
> their steak!* Moira Jones echoed Norman: *'we were
> reasonably lucky because my Grampfer worked in
> Spears, [it sold] meat,... we used to get say liver,
> sausages, a bit of meat, so... a li'l extra came our
> way.'*[111]

Ida Lenner & Albert Woodford better known as Ida & Bert were Empire stalwarts. Ida had been one of the Lenner trio. Christine Woodford

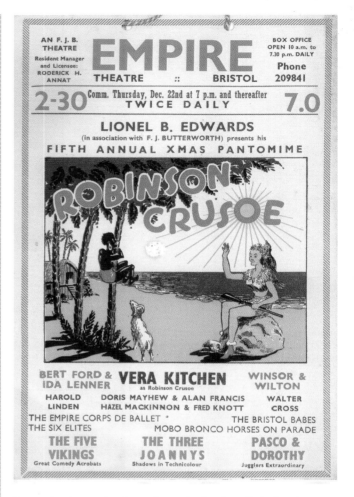

Pantomime's remained popular at the Empire, albeit risqué versions, up to its closure.

there, to meet young ladies...'[110] In winter the travelling fairgrounds retired to an area behind West Street.

The Empire offered a diverse programme packed with circus, music, comedy and drama which appealed to all generations. Continuing from the war, adults were drawn in by salacious shows such as '*Naughty Girls of 1947*', '*Peek-a-Boo*' featuring Phyllis Dixey and '*Venus was a Lady*.'[112]

Charley Plenty remembers his mother attending ballroom dances at the Drill Hall:

'A lot of people wouldn't remember Victor Silvester... he was a ballroom dance band leader and his tempo was renowned... she always tell me the tale when he was down there one day with his band...and she told me 'I danced with him down at the Drill Hall in Old Market and his breath smelt.'[113]

The Drill Hall was also used for Girl Guides, Trade Union meetings, boxing, arm-wrestling and as a postal office.

There were plenty of pubs for locals and visitors to frequent. The Palace Hotel was one of the most popular

with its six penny shots of gin and famous Ushers beers.

Methodist Central Hall hosted a range of classical music concerts delivered by musicians ranging from local pupils to the Royal Philharmonic.

For the union man and woman, Shepherd's Hall was still an important venue for meetings and speeches. While

Now flats, the Vestry Hall was a spit and sawdust alternative to the King's Cinema.

Kingsley Hall became the regional offices of the National Society of Painters, Amalgamated Union of Building Trade Workers, Bristol Trades Council, Bristol Borough Labour and the National Society of Operative Printers.

Old Market continued to be a street where every household item could be purchased. New shops moved into the street including piano manufacturer Mickleburgh's - and the renowned pram shop Hurwoods.[114]

The cluster of meat importers and wholesalers between numbers 51 and 54 formed Bristol's 'meat packing district.' There was also a wholesale Butcher in West Street – The West of England Meat Company. The local meat economy was given a further boost when Bristol pie and sausage manufacturer, Spears, moved to a new site in Broadplain in 1962.[115]

Bristol Rediffusion Ltd moved their head offices from Colston Street in the centre to 78 Old Market in 1947. Fourteen years later they opened a major store in 2-3 West Street.[116]

Prices matched local purchasing power. Bata's Old Market store sold shoes considerably cheaper than its Clifton store. Outfitters such as the 50 Shilling Tailor and from Weaver to Wearer provided quality suits at an affordable price.[117]

SWIMMING AGAINST THE TIDE

The hustle and bustle of Old Market masked an underlying decline. Its most prominent manifestation emerged from its isolation from the city.

Old Market had been part of a 'golden mile' of unbroken specialist shops. Now Castle Street was no more. In its place was a bomb site which Bristolians feared to cross, especially after dark. After the Second World War, Old Market became increasingly isolated and sidelined. The electric trams ceased operation in April 1941, when Halfpenny Bridge, next to the electricity generating station on Temple Back, was destroyed by bombs. In the 1950s, passenger trains to St Philips Station were diverted to Temple Meads – the station was eventually closed to passengers in 1953.

Mike Smith recalls working as a projectionist at the King's between 1967-1970:

The first double film I showed was 'Kinky Darlings' and 'Splendour in the grass' that was the only time when I was there that these type of films was shown. The real film which done well was 'Bullitt' Steve McQueen which was retained for a second week and then 'Till Death Do Us Part' the movie version of the TV series... The pay was very bad and the group was going through a bad spell and the commuting was taking its toll, so I decided to leave the Kings in early 1970 when I got married... The 'blue' reputation came after I left.[118]

Rosemary Dun describes visiting Aunt Maud in Old Market like going back in time.

The night time economy was most affected by the disconnection between Old Market and the city centre. But changes in the entertainment industry also went against the Street's venues. Theatre and television had now to compete with television. Television accelerated the decline in music hall and variety entertainment.[119] The Empire's only hope was to obtain a dramatic license with which it could compete with the Hippodrome or the Old Vic. But every application had been turned down over the years. With the death of manager Harry Day in 1939, its owners FJB Butterworth lost interest.

As early as 1945, FBJ Butterworth tried unsuccessfully to sell the Empire. Judging the tastes of the Empire audience had also become increasingly difficult to fathom. Audiences were variable, despite what was on stage. The only sure fire money spinner was pantomime, albeit a titillating version.

Fire damaged the Empire in February 1951. The building reopened without a Gallery and therefore a viable income. This and the news of the Council's redevelopment plans led to its closure. The Empire was bought by the BBC and used as a radio theatre.

The King's Cinema was also a victim of new industry practices and new technology. Old style large cinemas were now out of fashion and uneconomic. The trend was for the multiplex cinema – housing a number of smaller screens. When the nearby Tatler cinema closed, the King's Cinema took over its diet of sub-pornographic films. Indeed the last film shown at the Tatler was the unambiguously titled 'My Bare Lady.'

The King's may have secured a niche audience but it was, sadly, forever afterwards associated with sleaze. In the words of one interviewee 'It was dirty mac cinema.'[120]

THE HIGH RISE COMETH

The bombing of Britain's major cities presented the Government with an opportunity to undo centuries of unregulated development that had led to unhealthy slum conditions and to reconstruct along lines of a great new society. Planners were encouraged to think boldly 'the mood of the time was that experts, with confidence and enthusiasm, would create a totally new and better

Social Mobility

The Bristol Central Commercial College in Redcross Street helped many young men and women gain access to careers that were not open to their parents. Former police officer Bernie Mattock explained:

The subjects they taught [at Bristol Central Commercial College, Redcross Street] were shorthand typing, Pitman shorthand typing I could do, I wasn't bad at that.

These skills supported his move into office based work and from thence into the police force.[121]

The Farler Green Family

Below: Three generations of the Farler Green family who lived in St Phillips. The family members moved out of the area after the War.

Susan Green 1968 St Gregory's Horfield

Susan Green

Best Man Uncle Fred Farler

Mum, Grandma, & sister in law

Uncle Fred Farler in uniform

The demolition of the King's Cinema (FLHS)

Britain.'[122]

Slum clearance in St Jude's, Newtown, Easton and Barton Hill, accelerated after the War. New high flats, built in the 1950s, replaced back to back housing in Lamb Street, St Anne's and adjoining streets.

As with the pre-war slum clearance, local residents were relocated to the new suburbs of Knowle West, Hartcliffe and Withywood. The movement out of the area broke the relationship between the local community, the local economy and local institutions.

The economic boom also meant that a number of families could now afford to move out of an area which, while rich in culture was nonetheless seen as deprived. One interviewee sensed that her mother distanced herself from her mother who once lived in the neighbourhood.[123]

A change in aspirations also saw many young men and women take up new training opportunities which ultimately took them out of the area.

OLD MARKET V BROADMEAD

As early as 1943, Bristol's city planners mooted the idea of moving the city's centre to the North raising concomitant protest from those who understood what this would mean for Old Market.[124] A compromise of a kind was reached. Given the bombing of Castle Street and adjoining streets, the city's new retail centre became Broadmead. From 1950 onwards, Old Market was supplanted by the new shops and superstores which offered consumers everything under one roof. Old Market Street remained popular for some time owing to its specialist shops such as Hurwoods and 'off-the-peg' tailors but it felt increasingly cut off from modern shopping practices. The closure of the Jacob Street brewery in 1952 added to the impression that Old Market was no longer part of the new order. The site was largely cleared for the underpass – one wall, facing onto the ring road remains. Arguably the needs of the motorcar took precedence over the future for Old Market.

OLD MARKET V AUTOMOBILE

Although the M4 didn't reach the outskirts of Bristol until 1972, the opening of the M1 in 1959 had signalled the start of the motorway age and the dominance of the car in the urban landscape. It was a time when cars were king and the booming middle classes took to the road. From now on town planning was viewed through the car window. The issue was how to resolve the clash between people and cars.

Cary's Lane Silencing Public Inconvenience

The underground toilets, lit by glass panels set in the pavement, in the middle of the street opposite the Kings Cinema, were filled-in during 1966.[125]

The White Hart and Empire were among the many properties lost in the redevelopment. (FLHS)

The Bunch of Grapes & Don Cafe (pictured) were both knocked together, during the 1970s, to create the Old Market Tavern. (FLHS)

The 1966 Development Plan aimed – so it was claimed - to preserve and protect the city's historic buildings with the designation of special control areas. Old Market Street didn't feature however, being viewed as a 'Primary Distributor Road.'[126] The 1966 Development Plan also recommended filling-in the docks and building an urban expressway through them!

At the west end of Old Market a development plan was prepared. 'Included in the scheme are multi-storey

Model of the 1966 Old Market Redevelopment Plan

car parks, shops, a cinema, an hotel, offices and flats, all linked by pedestrian ways and elevated decks and footbridges across the Inner Circuit Road and across lower Castle Street to Castle Mound.'[127]

Central to this proposal was the construction of a two-tier roundabout. However, rather than link Old Market with Castle Park and Broadmead, this new intersection

Bristol 'Then & Now' captures the change in **Old Market** (Bristol Then & Now)

only increased the sense of isolation.

In order to build the Old Market roundabout, the Council made a compulsory purchase of ten properties including the Bunch of Grapes, The White Hart and the Brewery.

Within half a dozen years the 'high street' atmosphere of Old Market Street had disappeared. Forty premises (numbers 1 - 18 and 74 – 95) were lost to the development of the Ring Road. These included the Empire, the bakers, the grocers,the fruiterers, the White Hart and the Bunch of Grapes pubs, the Star Coffee House among many other legendary spaces.

The new roundabout, with its maze of pedestrian walkways, only increased the sense of isolation. Experience now shows that people are reluctant to use underpasses; and the escalators were frequently – and then permanently – made out of action.

A mile away to the east, over 150 buildings were demolished to make way for the Barton Hill roundabout (1973).[128] West Street also suffered a similar major reversal with the introduction of a one-way traffic system turning it from shopping street to 'traffic corridor.'[129] Old Market's role as an important thoroughfare was moved from being a blessing to becoming a curse.

Footfall through the area decreased in line with the increasing use of the motorcar.

DECLINE AND REGENERATION 1967-2015

he reconstruction of the City Centre spelt the end of Old Market as a major shopping area. One retailer explained:

'Basically, when they started the underpass, at our end of Old Market Street, down by the Evening Post Building, that basically cut Old Market Street off from Broadmead and trade took an absolute dive.'[130]

Retailers also consider parking restrictions as another major disincentive to shopping in Old Market:

'We were one of the shops sort of amongst them, they all went, again I think that was partly because the wardens wouldn't even let them stop their lorries outside to load the meat up. I mean it was so aggressively restrictive. Umm and there was us, we had customers go out and find their cars had been towed, Hurwoods eventually closed down.[131] In sum: *'It all went like a waste land''*[132]

Old Market had been sacrificed to the needs of the automobile. Rows and rows of boarded up shops along Old Market provided a perfect corridor for flyposting and indeed some Bristolians recall coming down to Old Market to find out about the latest gigs.

GRAND CLOSURES

If the first decades of the 20th century saw the opening of venues that placed Old Market firmly on the map, the latter half of the century saw a distinct reversal in this trend.

The Empire, now used as a BBC theatre, was demolished in 1965 to make way for the construction of the inner Ring Road.[133]

The Kings Cinema meanwhile closed on 4 December

The sorry state of the King's Cinema prior to the redevelopment of the site. (FLHS)

1976 with an X-rated double bill of 'Hot Dreams' and 'Man Hungry'. Once closed, the building became an eyesore that added another blight upon an already wretched landscape. The cinema was eventually demolished in 1981 and subsumed into the King's House development adjacent to the Old Market Roundabout.

Across the roundabout, the new Holiday Inn Complex contained The Europa Cinema. This cinema lasted from 1973, the year of the hotel's opening, until 1987.

THE END OF THE MISSION?

Of all the grand closures in Old Market, the local churches were among the most noticeable.

Colin & Mary The last wedding at Holy Trinity Church.

Old Market's various churches were radically affected by the area's changes. Local clergy worked hard, albeit in isolation from one another, to win new members to their congregations but were, for the most part, unsuccessful.

HOLY TRINITY CHURCH
The 'Cathedral of the East' was hit hard by the dispersal of its nearby communities. By the time of its closure Trinity's congregation had dwindled to a dozen or so regular worshippers. A new lease of life seemed possible from the emergence of a young evangelical fellowship led my Malcolm Widdecombe.[134] But tensions between the older worshippers, partly due to styles of worship, led the young Christians to look elsewhere. They were welcomed in by the congregation of St Philips and St Jacobs.[135] The young evangelicals were a major factor in the Church's revival. Holy Trinity meanwhile, closed in 1977 and has since enjoyed a new lease of life as

Malcolm Widdecombe

an arts and community centre.

Ironically, it was in fact St Philips & St Jacobs which was first earmarked for closure by the diocese. By 1960, huge maintenance costs and a small, mainly elderly congregation led the diocese to announce its intention to close the church at the end of 1964. The congregation thought otherwise and appealed against the Bishop's decision. Taking as their motto Matthew 6:33 they understood 'seeking first God's kingdom' to mean a programme of evangelism at home, and mission abroad. This in tandem with the arrival of young evangelicals gave the local church a new lease of life. The church was rebranded 'Pip n' Jay' and continues to thrive as a vibrant Christian community. The Church of St Jude's went into rapid decline from the 1960s. It was made redundant in 1990 and subsequently converted to flats in the 1990s by Knightstone Housing Association.

The Easton Christian Family Centre (ECFC) has become the major Church of England presence in the area. The ECFC combined the congregations of Holy Trinity, St Gabriel's (Lawrence Hill) and St Jude's and opened in1976.[136]

Reverend Phillip O.Dell's evangelical campaigns in the 1960s could not stop the decline in numbers at the Methodist Central Hall. Typically, the congregation were unable to support the cost of maintaining the vast building. From as early as 1963, the Hall's trustees were looking to dispose of the building whilst maintaining a worship

Interior of the Central Hall before its redevelopment.

presence of some kind. But potential buyers came and went unable to agree a price. The congregation ceased to meet on the site in 1982. It was occupied for a time by Bristol Cyrenians and was used as a shelter for the destitute.

Negotiations between the Trustees and various groups continued. Among the diverse plans for the use of building, one was put forward by the Central Hall Trust Committee. Formed between 1984-85, its members included the actresses Jill Truman and Liz Phalae, local businessman Phil Morris and John Winston - the son of

Bristol's most famous photographer, Reece Winston.[137] They proposed to transform the Hall into a 'theatre in the round', a restaurant and shops. Had this been successful, Old Market would have retained a flagship venue that reconnected the area to the local arts economy. However, the Trust were outbid by a property developer. In 1988 plans were approved for its conversion into 42 flats at a cost of £1.2m. The auditorium was demolished to make

Top: Old Market with the popular Man Tung, restaurant, far left, in view. Bottom: Methodist Central Hall's between closure and redevelopment. (Paul Bradburn)

way for the car park. Only the facade remains.[138]

In 1985 the Ebenezer chapel closed and became an architectural salvage business. The building was demolished during the 2014 May Bank Holiday. Plans had been mooted to transform the Central Hall into a theatre and music venue but these fell through amidst some controversy.

By contrast with its Protestant neighbours, St Nicolas

of Tolentine has flourished since the War. This is perhaps due to its critical importance to Irish migrants coming into East Bristol.

Whatever one's religious persuasion the decline of local churches had a deleterious impact upon the vitality of the community. Sunday schools, choirs, men's and women's groups had provided opportunities for the local community.

The closure of the local churches broke the link with the schools. But to an extent this relationship had already been reconfigured. The senior years at Hannah More School, for example, had moved to the former Barleyfields school on New Kingsley Road. The lower years moved in 1963.[139] The school was eventually demolished in 1979 to make way for a new Trinity Road police station. Once again St Nicolas of Tolentine retained close ties with the Church nearby.

NEW ARRIVALS

Of course it was not all doom and gloom. This period of decline did see some significant new employers come into the area. They included a bookmakers, a football pools agent, Practical Credit Services and an estate agent. There was also the Man Tung Chinese restaurant.

Bristol Evening Post and Western Daily Press wanted a highly visible prestige building to house the offices and the print hall. The purpose-built offices were constructed between 1970 and 1974.

'CASUALTY'

From 1986, the long-running and popular BBC series 'Casualty' was filmed in an anonymous-looking building on the Kingsland Trading Estate, off St Philips Road. Production was transferred to Cardiff in August 2011.

In the year or two before the move to Cardiff another St Philips Rd unit between the main set-up and the Art Department was also rented for housing 'set builds', despite its close proximity to the waste transfer railway

Radical Eyes set abroad

Shorn of its major venues, one might think that the area became introspective. However Old Market remained a vital space for radical activism albeit now focused on international conflict, in particular with the campaign to end apartheid. The birth of Bristol's anti-apartheid movement can be traced to a meeting between local activists and veteran campaigner Joe Slovo. From the 1960s to the 1990s Old Market became a focal meeting point for groups opposed to apartheid. Campaigns against apartheid brought together churches, students, and a broad array of leftist groups. They met variously at the Friends Meeting House St Jude's, the Central Hall, [prior to its closure], Kingsley and Shepherd's Hall respectively.

Bristol and thereby Old Market, was an important component in the anti-apartheid struggle. In 1987, Bristol's campaigners were visited by representatives from the South West Africa People's Organisation (SWAPO) and the African National Congress (ANC) at a meeting held in Shepherd's Hall.[140]

Dave Spurgeon, Secretary of the South Africa Resource Centre recalls one such meeting visited by the veteran ANC campaigner, Ronnie Press. Ronnie shared his memories of the anti-apartheid struggle of the ANC and its most famous leader. Following a Freedom Charter protest in 1955, he recalled that after 3-4 hours, the spyhole on his cell opened and his warder said your solicitor is here and in walked Nelson Mandela.' Ronnie later became a veteran of the famous 1950s treason trial with Nelson Mandela.[141]

The former family store at No 6 West Street became the offices and shop of the charity South African Resource Centre. The shop had been given to the charity in 1989 on 'a peppercorn rent' by Bristol City Council.[142]

Southern Africa Resource Centre

siding!.

A yard to the rear of the units opposite the studio warehouse also became rented for garage purposes and the ambulances etc. This was next to National Windscreens.'[143]

Old Market had, since the 1960s, become increasingly known for its food outlets. The Man Tung was a popular Chinese restaurant on the street. Chief Inspector Norman Pascal, remembers the Man Tung restaurant fondly. 'Once a year we would have our restaurant meal. Our mother would have proper Chinese food and we would have chicken and chips we were so English.[144] The record shop Rubber Soul, no 83 West Street was also a major draw for young people into the area.

DAY LIFE & NIGHT VICE

The idea that Old Market went into terminal decline after the Ring Road masks a more complex picture. One might argue that the street reverted to its 19th century extremes of Vice and Virtue.

Deprivation and alcoholism remained a feature of life in St Jude's. Beverley Douglas is one of many who recall the prevalence of homelessness in the area: 'The interesting thing is those people [rough sleepers] seemed

Casualties Location Manager Rob Champion

❝ *Our main Casualty warehouse units were in St Philips Road and were the last four on the left heading up from Midland Rd.*

The BBC scenic workshop was sited in Wadehurst Industrial Park, further up St Philips Rd until that and Make-up and Costume were privatised during the 1990s. Eventually a props store and art department was set up in Wadehurst, but I wasn't around at that exact time. They had been sited in the adjacent unit to the studio until the studio set expanded to occupy two units. The original middle unit was always for offices - stacked Portakabins - and canteen area, then when Editorial came from London, the 4th unit [nearest Midland Rd] also became stacked with more Portakabins for offices, artists' dressing rooms and the costume department. ❞

Street art under the Old Market underpass (Tony Gill)

all to be grown-ups – as opposed to young people – falling about in the road.[145] Illegal drugs increasingly joined alcohol as a cause of homelessness.

The empty spaces offered shelter to transient marginal figures.

'You'd get places boarded up. Lots of buildings would have people living in them. Years ago it wasn't called squatting, it was just people finding somewhere to sleep and move on. There wasn't such a big hype about people living in commercial premises.'[146]

Small pubs and clubs became the main focus of Old Market's night time economy. Echoing former associations, they were known locally as hangouts for petty criminals and hard men.

Local businessman Phillip Morris gives a colourful account of his first visit to the Gin Palace in the early 80s:

'I met this piano player V...he was a fantastic piano player...I thought what's going on here. Two coppers standing outside in uniform and not drinking and closing time come, they walk over to him and arrested him and took him out instead of arresting him there and then they let him finish...[he was a shoplifter]'

He further recalled a usual occurrence at the Long Bar:

'You'd get two fellas knockin' 'ammer dong 'ammerin' seven bells out each other in Old Market then they'd come in and have a drink cause they'd had an argument about something.' Balanced against these memories are those of meeting Acker Bilk in the Long Bar or listening to Adge Cutler 'singing away' in the Gin Palace' while 'V.. played piano.' [147]

But despite its reputation, former officers recall a traditional respect for the police which had begun to fade elsewhere:

'Next to the King's was a club - the 99 club. You'd

get a lot of villains going in there..it was open almost 24 hours – a lot of wheelin' and dealin' receiving stolen goods - property and stuff.'

Yet for all its drama during these years, former police officers agree that: Old Market was 'always, very, very quiet.' Officers on night patrol were mainly involved in checking to make sure that shops and offices had not been burgled during the night.[148]

Old Market's isolation opened a space in which new cultures and subcultures emerged.

Club Creme (pictured right) was one of Bristol's first table dancing venues. A gay bar also operated on the same premises. The club is now known as Temptations. (Tony Gill)

Old Castle Green, Gloucester Lane

" Suddenly Mary Ann and I were asked if we wanted to run our own pub, The Old Castle Green, in Old Market. Old Market at that time, 1978, was off the map. It was the winter quarters of a travelling fair, full of drunk Irishman and Scotsmen, failed petty thieves and old age pensioners. It was weird, but a chance to do what we wanted, stock my own juke box with my music, have my own bar billiards table and cook Mexican/Cajun food (not easy with what was available back then!)

We were around the corner from Biggles Music, one of the unsung heroes of the music scene then, so it wasn't long before they started coming in for lunch, 'just the one before I go home.' Next bands started coming in to eat and drink and be amused by the best juke box in Bristol. Soon enough someone (think it was Crazy Trains) asked if they could play one night, we said sure, but we can't pay you much, and there we go. It wasn't long before we had live music a couple of nights a week.

I had old contacts in the folk world so one night was folk; often Steve Payne, Jim Reynolds, Alamo or other local talent, but every few weeks a name who was passing through and stayed the night and played, people like Bert Jansch, John Martyn, Cliff Aungier and John Renbourn. The interesting thing was that most of the two audiences stayed for each other's gigs, which resulted in some interesting crossovers later.

Bristol was very like a number of villages back then, don't know if it is now, and that had a huge effect on the bands. Once Trinity opened up we became a regular watering hole before gigs and many people discovered us. Venue starting up around the corner also made a difference [formerly Bristol's main listing magazine]. Suddenly there were Electric Guitars and Exploding Seagulls on the scene and I remember also the insanity of the Spics early gigs.[149] "

TRINITY CENTRE

Following its closure in 1977, Holy Trinity Church was purchased by Bristol's African Caribbean Association. The Association were looking for a venue where they could deliver vocational and artistic training as a means to combat high youth unemployment. In reality it became best known as a music venue, used in particular by reggae and punk acts.

(Left) The Stingrays, supporting U2, 1979.
(Right) The Zen Hussies 00s

RED LIGHT ZONE

The Tatler and the King's Cinema in its latter years began the association between Old Market and vice. However, it was during the 1970s and '80s that this association deepened. Since 1979 there has been a licensed adult shop on West Street. A decade later the family firm next door moved from carpet seller to adult entertainment store. Massage parlours opened on Midland Road, Redcross Street and Old Market.

Most recently Old Market became the site of Bristol's first lap dancing club 'Club Crème'. This was despite

Tatler Cinema, Cary's lane, 1950s rival to the Kings Cinema

(Paul Townsend twitter.com/brizzlebuff)

Sex Worker: anonymous

The sex worker gave the following account of working in the West Street parlour during the late 1970s.

> The women with whom I worked indoors were like just a variety of women, younger women, they were just out of school. They normally worked in banks. The woman I worked with worked in a bank... she needed to top up her wages; It was mostly mothers... Different ages, I was probably one of the oldest ones... Black women, White women, Asian women, all mixed up, not Asian women from India, Asian women from China.

Her reflections on her experience challenge mainstream views of sex work:

> My life changed and my whole family's life changed from wandering from how you are going to pay the bills, you just had to get by,....to be able to go to the supermarket... get a trolley load of food and be able to pay the bills and be able to go on holiday and eventually I shared the car with somebody, you know its only me you dont need the whole car frankly... everything became manageable, we could have a holiday, we never ever had holidays, even in the old times when I was married I've never had a holiday. So we used to go camping...we did more than that... we used to go abroad... you know... so the children were raised with... you know doing things, everybody else... other kids did, suddenly they could go on sports trips.[150]

One can but ponder if similar views existed among the sex workers of St Judes generations previously. These generations are for the most part silent: they speak to us only through the eyes of officialdom.

considerable opposition from community and feminist groups.

The sex Industry, as shown previously, was not unique or new to Old Market. On-street sex work was particularly prevalent in St Paul's and Easton while a number of parlours are dotted along Bristol's major arterial roads but what is unique is the density, visibility and longevity of sex-related industries in the area. It is this that has given Old Market its most recent reputation.

REGENERATION:
A 'GAY QUARTER?'

Today Old Market is associated with its gay community but this is a relatively recent development. One can only speculate as to the presence of a gay community prior to

© Tony Gill www.tonygillphotography.co.uk

Aled Richards on holiday. Aled was 'the first Bristol man known to die of an AIDs related illness. (Terrence Higgins Trust & Richards Family)

- **1977** Gemini Sauna 56 West Street
- 'Following the lead of the Aled Richards Trust in 1996 new ventures started opening.'[152]: Village (Cottage) Sauna, Friends of Dorothy (1997), Castros (1998).
- **October 1996:** Lesbian Gay and Bi-sexual Forum hosted by Aled Richards Trust.
- **November 1996:** Living Room Project – support group for those living with HIV/Aids at 8-10 West Street.
- **July 1997:** Gay Men's Project at 8-10 West Street becomes a partner in the national CHAPS (Community HIV/Aids Prevention Scheme) scheme promoting safe sex.
- **July 1997:** Friends of Dorothy, Bristol's first lesbian and gay café opens at 48 Old Market Street.[153]
- As suggested by the creation of the Bristol Forum the 1990s, this was also a period of growing confidence and thereby increased visibility among Bristol's gay community.
- **September 1997:** Bristol held its first Pride event consisting of a parade from Castle Green to the Trinity Centre. Entertainment included bands, stalls and line dancing.
- **October 1997:** Support groups for young people: The Young Men's Group and The Coming Out Group established at the Aled Richard's Trust (ART). ART funding increased from £13,000 in 1986 to £327,000 in 1998/99.[154]

the 1970s. Homosexuality had only been decriminalised in 1967, thus much research needs to be done to uncover the layers of Bristol's gay history. Furthermore, behind the story of Old Market's gay community lies a complex relationship between the sex industry, the fetish scene and other groups. As one respondent explained:

'Old Market is the place to go where if you're gay or if you're into fetish, if you're into partners [partner swapping].'[151] At a time when British sexual morality was somewhat conservative, these differing lifestyles and interests shared a common need for discretion, security and freedom from judgement. Old Market's isolation

offered the perfect milieu.

However, it was the gay community which became the most prominent of the sexual minorities in Old Market. Bristol's gay venues - the Elephant, the Griffin, Oasis-

A Place for Everyone (Andy & Mandy www.phase8photos.com)

At home in the Gin Palace

> *One of the places I heard of, which a lot of people were going on about was Old Market. In particular the Palace, you've got to park your car and totter up the street in heels with taxi ranks and like that you're extremely nervous..but then you don't get a second glance.. you walk in there and it's all smiling faces and a warm, pink, red gold glow and it's just very welcoming and that's the thing I've always had - you know. Going upstairs and seeing all the Womad pictures - it's just very welcoming.*[155]

As the above suggests the great appeal of the Palace lies in its inclusivity.

> *The Palace had something unique. No matter who you were, or what you looked like, or whatever you were, you were welcomed by all the people in there, and it was really a nice place you could go, and no matter who walked through the door, whether you're Superman or a tramp. One day I was there and there was a lady in her mid-forties with no top on at all, just sitting, having a conversation with an old man opposite and no one batted an eyelid. That's the Palace and the randomness of it.*[156]

The drag Queens enjoy the passing of the Olympic flame 2012.

were traditionally located in the central areas.[157]

According to several commentators, Old Market's 'out' gay presence can be traced to the move by the Aled Richards Trust from Colston Street to Nos 8-10 West Street in 1992. The Trust was an HIV/AIDs prevention charity parallel to the Terrence Higgins Trust with which it merged in 2000.[158]

Its then worker, diversity activist Berkeley Wilde recalls his surprise at the paucity of services and activities for gay men and women in Bristol having come from London. He helped to set up and encourage a range of other services:

'*We wrote an application to the national lottery. This is 1996 now. And we were awarded £140,000! Which was incredible for a lesbian and gay youth project. We were the first in the country to be awarded that.*'

'*A lot of this work came from the HIV prevention strategy.*'

'*The Old Market scene started to develop in the late 90s, early noughties. And so there were new venues popping up. Certainly things like the Old Market Tavern and ones that are down towards Old Market Street have been much more recent in terms of development.*'[159]

By 2000, there was now a core group of shops, cafes, bars, clubs and a sauna. In recent years new venues have begun to cater to the needs of particular subcultures within the gay community. On the corner of

West Street is the venue 'Bristol Bear Bar'. As the name suggests, the bar caters to men who are attracted to a more masculine, hirsute appearance. The owners of the Bear Bar bought the lease and reopened the Gin Palace in 2008 on the understanding that it would be a gay friendly venue. It has, in fact, become a major venue for Bristol's drag and trans community. The Gin Palace in turn has now become a meeting point and a beacon for men who dress as women or who are in the process of gender reassignment.

The LGBT community presence appeared to move from strength to strength when a 900 capacity club opened on the site of the Lloyd's Branch on West Street. Flamingoes or as it was more popularly known, JustWins or Winns helped to drive 'footfall' along West Street.

By the late 90s, some commentators were beginning to describe Old Market as Bristol's 'gay village.' Some have greeted this idea with a degree of scepticism, especially when the strip is compared with Brighton and Manchester. Unlike Canal Street in Manchester, there is still little support for commercial ventures from the Council. Not everyone within the gay community has trumpeted the idea of a gay village. In a study of Bristol's night life, some men and women expressed concerns that a gay village would be a way of ghettoizing the community - others felt that Old Market was generally 'unsafe' and would be even more so for gay men and women.[160]

Be that as it may, the impact of the gay community as a regenerating force cannot be disputed.

CHARITIES

Church decline did not end faith based charitable work in Old Market. The Methodists maintained their Midland Road shop presence as part of their ongoing support to society's most vulnerable.

However, in many regards, secular bodies came to replace and duplicate the pre-war work done by the

Guild of the Handicapped (twitter.com/brizzlebuff)

churches. Bristol Municipal Charities and the Bristol City Council retained ownership of a number of properties on Old Market and West Street. As with the South African Resource Centre, a number of empty properties were leased to Bristol charities such as the Women's Centre, Barnardos, and the mental health charity, Mind.

From the 1980s onwards Bristol's trade union organisations moved out of Kingsley Hall. The building is now used by a charity supporting young people facing homelessness.

The concentration of offices has contributed to the area's revival. Derelict shops are back in use as studio, business, and flats.

GUILD OF THE HANDICAPPED

In the 1990s the building that housed the Guild of the Handicapped became a Bristol City Council Area Office.

NEW RESIDENTS

A new diverse community has moved into the area taking advantage of the flats above the retail outlets, and the conversion of existing buildings. Barstaple House for example was sold by Bristol Municipal Charities in 2010 and converted into private flats. Other residential schemes such as the flats built behind the Methodist Hall

The Olympic flame comes to Old Market.

and the conversion of the Drill Hall have all played a part in diversifying the income, educational, and occupational profile of the local community in recent years. Local residents feel, however, that there is still need for more family housing with open space.[161]

ETHNIC MINORITY REGENERATION

One of the most significant transformations in the area is its growing ethnic diversity. In keeping with the national pattern of post-war urban migration, ethnic minorities have increasingly become a replacement population in Britain's inner city, in particular within East Bristol. According to the 2001 census, the Old Market Quarter has a significant black and minority ethnic (BME) population of 42.6% compared to the Bristol average of 16%. In Bristol's new communities – East African &

Eastern European migrants are particularly prominent among the Quarter's BME population.[162] Many have come to occupy the flats on the site of the back-to-back housing once inhabited by White working class migrants from rural England.

As such the area is one of the most dynamic barometers of globalisation in action. Yet migrants have done more than just taken up residence. A century earlier, Amos Raselles was one of a handful of ethnic minority shop owners. In the 21st century, the retail community around Old Market hails from every corner of Africa, the Middle East, East and Central Europe. This trend began with a number of Greek-Cypriot owned restaurants in the 1970s, but has increased in recent years.

In a striking historical volte-face, the former Redcross school has, since 2005, become an Islamic school. The Andalucia Academy which caters for primary girls and boys and secondary girls, is run by Bristol Islamic Schools Trust (BIST).[163]

CONSERVATION

The influx of new comers has energised the area but, arguably, it is architectural heritage that has given weight to calls for its regeneration.

Dorothy Brown

The preservation of Old Market's heritage sites might not have occurred were it not for the indefatigable Dorothy Brown. (1927-2013)[164] Dorothy is widely regarded as the saviour of Old Market.[165] She established the Bristol Visual and Environmental Group, in response to the unveiling of the 1966 Bristol Development plan. Through her efforts, nearly all the 400 buildings earmarked for demolition under the plan, including those in Old Market, were saved from destruction. Dorothy's campaigning went beyond the area to cover heritage sites throughout Bristol and the South West. Her son Guy is quoted as saying: 'She was a born campaigner. If she saw something needed doing, she would be the first to the barricades, and was never so happy as when organizing a fight or fixing a leaking roof.'[166]

Inside Skin Deep Tattoo parlour West Street.
(Tony Gill www.tonygillphotography.co.uk)

With mounting concern for the state of the buildings, Old Market Street – including West Street - was recommended in 1979 as a Conservation Area.[167] 47 buildings in the area were listed as being of historical interest. With this designation there was an opportunity to apply for Grant Aid. It was noted that most of the properties were used for retail purposes, but with the upper floors remaining vacant.

COMMUNITY COHESION?

According to the 2011 Census the population of the Old Market Quarter stood at 4,620 which represents a significant increase from 2000 residents recorded by the previous census.[168] This makes it one of the City Centre's fastest growing residential areas. Its population is expected to increase further as it also has one of the lowest population densities in the City Centre.

As we have discussed the diversity of the Quarter is unique in Bristol. Given such an eclectic mix of cultures and lifestyles, Old Market might seem to be a recipe for

The Empire Returns

The short life of the new Empire illustrates the fragility of Old Market's recovery. The fillip given to West Street with the opening of Winns stalled with the closure of the club in 2011. West Street seemed to receive a life line when creative producer Keda Breeze reopened the venue in 2013 as a cabaret and theatre space. In name and spirit, the club revived memories of its predecessor. However the new Empire closed due to licensing issues in less than a year.[169]

(Taphouse)

atomization, yet the opposite appears to be the case. As one respondent explained:

'We all respect each other... every walk of life... we respect them in their walk of life and they respect us in our walk of life.'[170]

ONE VOICE FOR OLD MARKET

Formed in 2011, The Old Market Community Association (OMCA) have brought together residents, traders, and landlords from across the diverse communities. It has pressed the Local Authority to invest energy and capital in humanizing the area. There is much to be done. Some Bristolians still see the area purely in terms of vice: traffic and pollution are ever present and there is not a single tree along Old Market. Buildings remain empty, turn-over of retail premises is high, and upturns are easily reversed.

Achieving cohesion in Old Market is a fragile balancing act. Keen to move away from its association with the 'the dark edge of town', some traders and residents have opposed the presence and certainly the proliferation of the red light district in Old Market.[171]

The area has been a battle ground for differing attitudes to sex and sexual freedom. In 2000 the Archbishop of Canterbury rebuked the organisers of Bristol fetish night Spank for using the Trinity Centre for a party night. For some, including the archbishop, the night had insulted the heritage of the building. Others might argue it had allowed a space for free expression.

Opposition to plans for another lap dancing club was, in fact, an important spur to the formation of the Community Association.

Struggles such as these expose the sharply conflicting views of the areas present and future. Underpinning these perspectives are a wealth of divergent lifestyles each claiming Old Market as home. In this regard the area echoes the 'cheek by jowl' coexistence between mainstream and marginal existence - between Vice & Virtue - that existed decades earlier.

Portraits of Old Market residents 2015. Clockwise from top left: Bo, Juan, Julian & Buba, Bobbi. (Andy & Mandy www.phase8photos.com)

ENDNOTES

1 Brown D. 1979, Bristol Castle and the Old Market Area, Bristol, p.5.

2 Christine. 2014 'Analysis of 1901 & 1911 census data' p.12: Bristol Archeological Society Brown D. 1981, Bristol and How it Grew, Bristol, p.19.

3 Bristol City Council Old Market Character Appraisal Conservation Area 16 2008

4 Mathews W. 1794, Bristol Guide, p. 43.

5 Visitors Guide to Bristol, (undated. 1960s) p.64.

6 Interview With Tony Dyer 1st December 2014

7 Jennings H.J. 1872, Bingham's Guide to Bristol, Bristol, p.160.

8 See also http://en.wikipedia.org/wiki/Palace_Hotel%2C_BristolOakley, M., 2006, Bristol Railway Stations 1840 – 2005, Redcliffe Press, Bristol, p.97.

9 www.architecturaldecor.co.uk/blogs/architectural-decor/8889635-a-little-bit-of-chicago-in-bristol

10 Waifs and Wanderers in St Jude's', The Homes of the Bristol Poor by the Special Commissioner of the Bristol Mercury (Bristol, William Lewis & Sons, 1884), p.26.

11 see also https://www.flickr.com/photos/brizzlebornandbred/6290754671/in/photolist-azTLcr-ietpvH-i9nFR1-hZ7qHj-iFbj9P-j2KLC4-iqCokx-iBTaBU-jKgd2h-ipa6hz-ijD5mb-jRZ6Y6//www.independent.co.uk/news/uk/crime/amelia-dyer-the-woman-who-murdered-300-babies-8507570.html

12 The Centenary Report of Elm House: Home of Bristol Mission to Women and Girls (1955), p. 3 cited in The Bristol Female Mission Society, 1859-1884: Prevention or Cure? Gill James, PhD student, University of the West of England 2007

13 Eric, verbal testimony passed on to volunteer Sara Evans September 2014. Eric was a former resident of Bristol South almshouse.

14 Loxton S. 1992, Loxton's Bristol, Redcliffe Press, Bristol, p.46.

15 Waifs and Wanderers p34

16 Eric verbal testimony Redcross Alms House Eric passed on to volunteer Sara Evans September 2014

17 Reminiscence session 16th December 2014

18 http://maps.bristol.gov.uk/knowyourplace/

19 Jones C. Analysis of 1901 & 1911 census

20 See Malwyn, Edwards, Methodism and England (1943) for an in-depth study of the social role of Methodism in England.

21 Thompson George 'East Bristol History Group Chronicle The Streets and People of St Jude's pamphlet pp9-10

22 Williams J. and Humphries C. 2008, Mother Keeps a Mangle, Bristol, p.23

23 Interview with Jack Williams, 28th November 2014

24 2012 Reminiscence session reported by Mawusi Sokoni 3rd March 2015

25 Humphries S. 1983, Bristol's Other History, Bristol Broadsides, p.10.

26 Doreen Watkins Remembering Old Market Reminiscence Session 16th Tuesday 2014

27 Townsend Paul, The King's Cinema www.flickr.com/photos/brizzlebornandbred/2077515124/

28 Maldwyn L. Edwards, A Memoir of Lillian Davis Broadbelt (London:Epworth Press, 1937) cited in Angela Connelly Methodist Central Hall doctoral thesis p307

29 Interview with Audrey Dayer 13th June 2014

30 Methodist Central Hall Jubilee pamphlet

31 Verbal testimony Eric September 2014

32 Andrew Foyle Pevsner Architectural Guides, Bristol (New Haven: Yale University Press, 2004) p265

33 Roads, Nick, & Forman Dave, with Mike Mantin, The Guild Heritage Building Braggs Lane Bristol pamphlet pp6-7 (2011-2012)

34 Old Market Industrial Bristol Archeological Review Bristol Industrial Archeology Society p133

35 Ibid p133

36 Bristol Industrial Archaeological Society Empire Theater notes

37 The People's theatre in Bristol 1930-45 (1979) Our History Series No 72 BRO 40214/2/3/3/

38 Harrison D. 2002, Bristol Remembered, Tempus Publishing, Stroud, p.48.

39 Interview with Lynn & Kenneth Mitchell. Lynn's mother went to school with Cary Grant 14th October 2014 see also Doris Crane (nee Jarett)'s memories of a young Cary Grant http://www.bbc.co.uk/history/ww2peopleswar/about/siteinformation.shtml

40 Hallet T. 2002 Bristol's Forgotten Empire: The History of the Empire Theater, Chapters 2-3

41 Ibid p.69

42 Ibid p.97

43 Humphries S. 1983 Bristol's Other History, Bristol Broadsides, Bristol, p.77.

44 Arrowsmith's Dictionary of Bristol (1906) cited in Bristol Archaeological Society Notes

45 BRO/32080/TC8/1/18 Leaflet

46 Bristol Record Office 32080/TC5/4/1

47 Bristol Industrial Archaeological Society notes

48 Humphries S. 1983, Bristol's Other History, Bristol Broadsides, p.37.

49 Humphries S. 1983, p.47.

50 McNeill J. 2012, Ben Tillett, Bristol Radical History Group.

51 Harrison D. 2002, Bristol Remembered, Tempus Publishing, Stroud, p.49.

52 Rosemary Nursery History Project 2014

53 Humphries S. 1983, Bristol's Other History, Bristol Broadsides, p.25.

54 Kelly's Bristol Directory, 1931.

55 Trinity Garden Party anonymous interviewee Trinity Garden Party 2014

56 Quoted in Samuel J. 1997, Jews in Bristol, Redcliffe Press, Bristol, p.166.

57 Hudson J. 2013, Adge - King of the Wurzels, Bristol Books, p.64.

58 Wright's Bristol Directory, 1901.

59 Malos E. 1983, Bristol Women in Action

60 Humphries S. 1983, Bristol's Other History

61 Western Daily Press, 23 December 1932.

62 Western Daily Press, 27 October 1936.

63 Western Daily Press, 14 August 1931.

64 BRO 32/080/TC9/4/6

65 BRO 32080 TC5/5/5 a-k

66 Ball Roger, Talk Bread and Batons The Old Market Riots 1932 Trinity Centre Bristol 24th June 2014

67 South Gloucestershire Gazette 27/2/2. Quoted in Blackwell, D. and Ball, R., 2012, Bread or Batons, Bristol Radical Pamphleteer Pamphlet #19, p.16.

68 Ibid, p.14.

69 Report by Inspector A Dyke, 10th February, Bristol Constabulary, Unemployed Demonstration, Bristol Record Office, POL/20/9/2

70 Ibid

71 Letter from H.E. Rogers to the Chief Constable, 11 February 1932, Bristol Record Office, POL/20/9/2

72 Letter from Josiah Green, Town Clerk, to H.E. Rogers, 18th February, Bristol Record Office, POL/20/9/2

73 South Gloucestershire Gazette 27/2/2. Quoted in Blackwell D. and Ball R. 2012, Bread or Batons, p.16.

74 Interview with Bill Curtis 11/11/1998. http://sounds.bl.uk/Accents-and-dialects/Millenium-memory-bank/021M-C0900X00510X-2600V1

75 Report by F.W. Hicks, Superintendant and Chief Clerk, undated, Bristol Record Office, POL/20/9/2

76 Letter from Maby to J Maxwell, 13 April 1932, Bristol Record Office, POL/20/9/2

77 International Labour Defense (Bristol Section), undate2014d (1932), Bread or Batons, London, p.6.

78 International Labour Defence (Bristol Section), undated (1932), Blackwell D & Ball R. Bread and Batons, p.16.

79 Interview with Jack Williams

80 Old Market Industrial Archaeology Review, (draft). p.9.

81 Bristol Central Reference Library Oral History Transcriptions. TWC 46 (Lois Cann)

82 Interview with Antony Peplar, 14th July 2014

83　Interview with V.A Hole, 28th February 2014

84　Interview with Charley Plenty 19th December 2014

85　Doreen Watkins Reminiscence Session 16th December 2014

86　Interview with Jack Williams 28th November 2014

87　Ibid

88　Thomas, Bill, Sixty Years on and still a Good Ideal, Bristol Record Office, 40018 (9), p.15.

89　Penny J. 2010, Bristol at War, Breedon Books, Derby, p.170.

90　Various, Edmead P. 1994, Dream on – Bristol Writers on Cinema, New Words, Bristol, p.69.

91　Bristol Central Reference Library Oral History Transcriptions. TWC 23 (Garry Atterton)

92　Race Wynn Neil. 2008, pamphlet 7 'Race War' Black American GIs in Bristol and Gloucestershire during World War 11, Bristol Radical History Group, p4.

93　Ibid p 5 -7.

94　Interview with Theodora Mighty 16th June 2014.

95　Bristol Central Reference Library Oral History Transcriptions. TWC 23 (Garry Atterton)

96　http://brisray.com/bristol/briot2.htm

97　Bristol Central Reference Library Oral History Transcriptions. TWC 23 (Garry Atterton)

98　Ibid

99　Interview with V.A Hole

100　Moira Jones, Bob Jones & Norman Gauter, 1st November 2014

101　Ibid

102　Ibid

103　Interview with Robert John Philip Rhodes 22nd June 2014

104　Interview with V.A Hole

105　1947 Anniversary Report cited in Sixty Years On Methodist Central Hall booklet

106　Interview with Audrey Dyer

107　Telephone Interview with Terrence Kelshaw 21st July 2010 cited in Culture and Change In Urban Bristol Edson Burton & Annie Berry Trinity Centre 2011 p3

108　Interview with Former residents Norman Gautier, Moira Jones, Bob Jones August 2014

109　Interview with Charley Plenty 19th December 2014

110　Ibid

111　Interview with Bob Jones, Moira Jones and Norman Gautier.

112　Terry Hallet, Bristol's Forgotten Empire Chapter 8 pp149-163

113　Interview with Charley Plenty 19th Dec 2014

114　Kelly's Bristol Directory, 1947. see also https://www.flickr.com/photos/brizzlebornandbred/4258666155/

115　Interview with Phillip Morris 19th November 2014

116　http://www.rediffusion.info/Bristol/

117　Bristol Industrial Archaeology Society &

118　Mike Smith email account 11th March 2015

119　Kathleen Barker, Bristol Branch of the Historical Association Bristol's Lost Empires Pamphlet n.d.

120　Interview with Philip Morris

121　Interview with Bernie Mattock 13th October 2014

122　Alison Ravetz, Remaking Cities (1980), Chapter 1. L. Esher, A Broken Wave. The Rebuilding of England 1940-1980 (Pelican ed., 1983), Chapter 1 cited in Junichi Hasegawa The Replanning of the Blitzed City Centre in Britain : A comparative study of Bristol, Coventry and Southampton 1941-1950 Doctoral thesis see also John Punter (1991) A microcosm of design control in post-war Britain: A case study of office development in central Bristol 1940–90, Planning Perspectives, 6:3, 315-347, DOI:

123　Interview with Rosemary Dunn 27th April 2014

124　John Punter (1991) A microcosm of design control in post-war Britain

125　Stephenson D. et al 2005, Old Market, Newtown, Lawrence Hill and Moorfields, Stroud, p.21.

126　Bennett J.B. 1967, Bristol of the Future, p.36.

127　Ibid, p.35.

128　Stephenson D. et al 2005, p.100.

139　Ibid, p.27.

130　Interview with Ted Fowler, 1st & 15th July 2014

131　Ibid

132　Interview with Robert John Phillip Rhodes 30th December 2014

133　Nichols P. 2007, The Last Empire, Bristol Review of Books, Issue 4, Autumn 2007.

134　Interview with Mervyn Evans 20th April 2010 cited in Edson Burton & Annie Berry What's Your Trinity Story

135　Interview with Terence Kelshaw

136　Ibid

137　Interview with Phillip Morris

138　Bristol Industrial Archeology site notes

139　Former pupil Colin Flickr https://www.flickr.com/photos/brizzlebornandbred/10462328365/in/photolist-gWwaHP-ikwKN6-jLYUoG-i9RgRb-jC5u26-ijD5mb-jAL9P3-bqk6wY-jNJ3nz-jQA1mg-5Wkz

140　BRO 4/2242/Adm//CO/3

141　Interview with David Spurgeon Secretary of the South Africa Resource Centre (SARC) 27th June 2014.

142　Interview with David Spurgeon see also SARC leaflet n.d.

143　Rob Champion Local Manager written testimony 13th January 2014

144　Conversation with Norman Pascal, 10th March 2014

145　Interview with Beverley Douglas 18th August 2014

146　Ibid

147　Ibid

148　Ibid

149　Mick Freeman reminiscences in http://www.

Remembering Old Market Reminiscence Session.

bristolarchiverecords.com/people/people_Mick_Freeman.html

150　Interview with anonymous sex worker, 22nd July 2014

151　Katie and Beau Interview 2nd October 2014

152　Howes R. Gay West, Silverwood Books, p.152.

153　Venue, 22 August, 1997.

154　Howes R. Gay West, Silverwood Books, p.154.

155　Interview with Andrew Hurdle on the 24th November2014

156　Ibid

157　Interview with Richard Jackson & Out stories, 12th November, www.outstoriesbristol.org.uk/timeline-1967-to-present

158　http://outstoriesbristol.org.uk/people/biographies/richards-aled/

159　Wilde, Berkeley, Talk 'Coming Out in Rainbow Colors' 9th July 2014 Trinity Centre

160　"Aubrey et al Youth Culture and Night Life in Bristol A Report. Centre for Urban and Regional Development Studies and Department of Sociology and Social Policy University of Newcastle upon Tyne NEI 7RU, UK pp76-77

161　Old Market Quarter Neighbourhood Development Plan, 2013, p.43.

162　Ibid, p10

163　Ibid, p10

164　Old Market Development Plan, p56

165　See Dorothy Brown 'Bristol Castle'

166　bristolpost.co.uk/Farewell-tireless-campaigner-Dorothy-Brown/story-19952415-detail/story.html

167　Planning and Traffic Committee, 15th August 1979, Old Market Conservation Area, Final Designation, Bristol.

168　Old Market Quarter Neighbourhood Development Plan

169　Keda Breeze 31st March 2014 http://www.bristolpost.co.uk/Check-burlesque-freakshows-dangerous-tea-Empire/story-1994565

170　Interview with Katie and Beau

171　Charles Chesney, former Chair of Old Market Community Association email account 10th March. www.bristolpost.co.uk/Check-burlesque-freakshows-dangerous-tea-Empire/story-1994565

SOURCES

WORKS CITED

Aldous T. 1979, *Changing Bristol*, Redcliffe Press for the Bristol Civic Society, Bristol.

Bennett J.B. 1967, *Bristol of the Future*, Bristol City Council, Bristol.

Blackwell D. and Ball R. 2012, *Bread or Batons*, Bristol Radical History Pamphlet #19.

Bolton D. 2011, *Made in Bristol*, Redcliffe Press, Bristol.

Brown D. 1979 Bristol Castle & Old Market area Pamphlet

Brown D. 1981, *Bristol and How it Grew*, Bristol Visual and Environmental Group, Bristol.

Burlton C. 2011, *Trenches to Trams*, Tangent Books, Bristol.

Dening C.F.W. 1943, *Old Inns of Bristol*, John Wright and Sons Ltd, Bristol.

Foyle A. 2004, *Pevsner Architectural Guides: Bristol*, Yale University Press.

Howes R. 2011, *Gay West*, Silverwood Books, Bristol.

Hudson J. 2013, *Adge - King of the Wurzels*, Bristol Books, Bristol.

Humphries S. et al 1983, *Bristol's Other History*, Bristol Broadsides, Bristol.

Mathews W. 1794, *Bristol Guide*, Bristol.

Oakley M. 2006, *Bristol Railway Stations 1840 – 2005*, Redcliffe Press, Bristol.

Penny J. 2010, *Bristol at War*, Breedon Books, Derby.

Samuel J. 1997, *Jews in Bristol*, Redcliffe Press, Bristol.

Stephenson D. et al 2002, *Old Market, Newtown, Lawrence Hill and Moorfields*, History Press, Stroud.

Thomas Bill, *Sixty Years on and still a Good Ideal*, Bristol Record Office, 40018 (9).

Williams J. and Humphries C. 2008, *Mother Keeps a Mangle*, Bristol.

Wright's *Bristol Directory*, 1901.

Wyn N.A. 2008, *'Race War' Black American GIs in Bristol and Gloucestershire during World War Two*, Bristol Radical History Pamphlets, Bristol.

Aubrey M et al. Report *Youth Culture and Night Life in Bristol* Centre for Urban and Regional Development Studies Policy University of Newcastle

Bristol City Council 2008 *Old Market Character Appraisal* Conservation Area

Bristol Industrial Archaeological Society The History of Old Market Street

Edwards M. 1943 *Methodism and England* Epworth Press London

Edwards M. 1937 *A Memoir of Lillian Davis Broadbelt* Epworth Press London

James G. 2007 PhD thesis *The Bristol Female Mission Society* 18859-1884

Jennings H J. Binghams 1872 Guide to Bristol

Hallet T. 2002 *Bristol's Forgotten Empire: The History of the Empire Theatre* Badger Press Wiltshire

Hannam J. *Bristol Independent Labour Party* Bristol Radial History Group Pamphlet #31

Harrison D. 2002 *Bristol Remembered*, Tempus Publishing Stroud

Hasegawa J. 1991 *The Replanning of the Blitzed City Centre in Britain* Doctoral thesis University of Warwick

Gillespie G. & Jones R. 2013 *The Naked Guide to Bristol* Tangent Bristol.

Loxton S. 1992 *Loxton's Bristol* Redcliffe Press Bristol

McNeil J. 2012 *Pamphlet Ben Tillet* Bristol Radical History Group #20

Methodist Central Hall booklet 1947 60 Years On

Nicolas P. (2007) *The Last Empire*, Bristol Review of Books Issue 4 Autumn.

Punter J. 1991 article *A microcosm of design control in post-war Britain*, Planning perspectives 6.3

Ravetez A. *1980 A Broken Wave: The Rebuilding of England 1940-1980* Pelican

Roads N. Forman D. 2011-12 *The Guild Heritage Building* Braggs Lane Bristol

Stephenson D. et al. 2005 Old Market, Newtown, Lawrence Hill and Moorfields Images of England series History Press Stroud

Thompson G. n.d. pamphlet The Streets and People of St Jude's

Various. Edmead E.P. 1994 Bristol Writers on Cinema, New Words Bristol

William Lewis. 1884 *The Homes of the Bristol Poor*

VICE & VIRTUE INTERVIEWS (INT), CONVERSATIONS, & REMINISCENCE SESSIONS

Written Testimony (email) Charles Chesney 11th March 2015

Int with Katie & Beau 2nd October 2014

Int with Audrey Dayer 13th June 2014

Int with Beverley Douglas 18th August 2014

Int with Rosemary Dunn 27th April 2014

Int with Tony Dyer 28th November 2014

Verbal testimony, Eric reported by Sara Evans 1st December 2014

Int with V.A.Hole 28th February 2014

Int with Andrew Hurdle 24th November 2014

Int with anonymous Garden Party 11th May 2014

Int with Richard Jackson 12th November 2014

Int with Bernie Mattock 13th October 2014

Int with Theodora Mighty 16th June 2014

Int with Norman Gautier Bob & Moira Jones & Moira Jones

Int with Lynn & Kenneth Mitchell 14th October 2014

Int with Philip Morris 19th November 2014

Conversation with Norman Pascal 10th March 2015

Int with Antony Peplar 14th July 2014

Int with Charley Plenty 19th December 2014,

Int with Robert John Philip Rhodes 30th December 2014

Int with David Spurgeon 27th June 2014

Written testimony Mike Smith 10th March 2015

'Remembering Old Market' Reminiscence Session, Doreen Watkins 16th December 2014

Int with Sex Worker anonymous 22nd July 2014

Reminiscence Session reported by Mawusi Sokoni 3rd March 2015

Int with Jack Williams 28th November 2014

Int Jean Erskine& Ann-Marie Vowles 20th March 2015

WEBSITES

Know your place
maps.bristol.gov.uk/knowyourplace/

The Changing Face of Bristol
www.bristolpast.co.uk

Brizzle Born and Bred: www.flickr.com/
photos/brizzlebornandbred/7280790592/in/
photostream/ see also www.flickr.com/photos/
brizzlebornandbred/6290754671/in/photolist-azTLcr-
ietpvH-i9nFR1-hZ7qHj-iFbj9P-j2KLC4-iqCokx-iBTaBU-
jKgd2h-ipa6hz-ijD5mb-jRZ6Y6//www.independent.
co.uk/news/uk/crime/amelia-dyer-the-woman-who-
murdered-300-babies

wikipedia

http://sounds.bl.uk/Accents-and-dialects/
Milleniummemory-bank/021M-C0900X00510X-2600V1

Insert http://www.rediffusion.info/Bristol/

Flickr

www.architecturaldecor.co.uk/blogs/architectural-
decor/8889635-a-little-bit-of-chicago-in-bristol

NEWSPAPERS

Bristol Post

Bristol Observer

Western Daily Press

ARCHIVES

Bristol Record Office, (BRO) & Bristol Central Library